The Psychic Science of Auras

"Visualize the human body as a transparent man-nequin which has the capability to transmit any colors from within itself, depending on how the 'occupant' is thinking or feeling."

—RAY STANFORD

Incredible though it may sound, this is how aura seer Ray Stanford sees people every day—with rings of color around all, or parts of their bodies. And they reveal not only medical problems, but individual characteristics (orange for pride, yellow for intellect) and immediate feelings (red for anger, blue for depression) as well!

In *What Your Aura Tells Me*, Ray Stanford tells you more about yourself and those around you than you might otherwise ever know—or even guess!

RAY STANFORD

WHAT YOUR AURA TELLS ME

A KANGAROO BOOK
PUBLISHED BY POCKET BOOKS NEW YORK

POCKET BOOKS, a Simon & Schuster division of
GULF & WESTERN CORPORATION
1230 Avenue of the Americas, New York, N.Y. 10020

*This book is dedicated
to an expanded awareness
of the entire spectrum
of human perception.*

Contents

Preface

The personal experiences related herein are described as best I know how. Use of words such as "aura" and "thought form" was necessary because they are widely accepted. I would have preferred terms that provide less of a preconceptual box into which to fit the strange things experienced. Nevertheless, I felt my adventure in seeing meaningful lights and forms around everyone must be told in a way accessible to all.

Perhaps, therefore, my scientific friends will forgive me for taking semantic liberties for the sake of simplified communication of some very intense and personal perceptions.

WHAT YOUR AURA TELLS ME

1

But Gee! That's What I See!

"Under natural conditions, women only display pink in their auras when they are pregnant. Rosy clouds of light seem to nestle about the lower abdomen of the mother-to-be. It usually begins within a matter of hours after conception.

"Of course," I added knowingly, "it *never* happens in men."

The group of distinguished psychologists and psychiatrists chuckled as one of them leaned forward.

"The pink, or the pregnancy, Mr. Stanford?" he asked with amusement.

"Look, take it from me. If you see a 'man' with a pink aura, you're really looking at a pregnant transvestite!"

That fact established, the next twenty minutes or so were taken up in my trying to explain what each of the other colors means when I see it in the human aura.

The immediate business, however, was for me to participate in the "informal experiment" of describing the aura of each University of Virginia researcher, and for me to deduce "something evidential" from it. My identical twin brother, Dr. Rex G. Stanford, a well-known psychologist and parapsychologist, had carefully set up the test in a way whereby I knew nothing about any of the persons gathered, not even their fields of education, training, or research.

"Thus," Rex said, "if you 'see' any background in the so-called aura around any one of them, we will at least know you did not get the information from anything I told you."

Slowly and with what confidence I could muster under such skeptical scrutinizing, I scanned the auras of all those present.

"Of course," I said, biding my time so as to locate the most intense and active aura in the group for an easy start, "I will read neither my brother's aura nor that of his wife. That would prove nothing. That which is not puzzling or challenging is of little interest to me, anyway."

To my right across the room sat a pleasant-looking man whom I guessed might be in his forties. He had been introduced as Bob Van de Castle, but his aura looked more interesting than either his face or the unusual name.

As spokesman for the group, Rex had told me, "None of us are convinced of the objective reality of what you call auras. However, we are scientifically interested in the whole spectrum of the human body and mind. So, in order that we may look at your claim to read auras in the context of what your 'aura awareness' can tell you about a person unfamiliar to you, please withhold *none* of your impressions from us. Even if you feel you see something quite personal, tell us everything."

It was precisely some of those "quite personal" things evident in Van de Castle's aura that caused me to choose his as the first one to read. So, after describing the colors and shapes involved, I slowly gave my interpretation of them, all the while searching his aura for further data that would prove convincing or evidential.

Suddenly I must have turned several shades of "blush"! Van de Castle said he noticed my jaw drop in astonishment.

Often things are seen around persons which I hesitate to reveal, for fear of embarrassing them—or else myself! But what I now saw, even considering all my years of aura seeing, was just too much to believe.

At first I told myself that it was impossible, I must be imagining it. "Better forget what you're seeing," I tried to convince myself. Then I remembered the axiom that I had so long applied and had advised all other persons studying their own psychic abilities to use: Say whatever comes to you without hesitation. It may not make sense to you, but it often *does* to the person you are "reading."

But, in view of my earlier remarks about the auras of pregnant women, how could I possibly get up the nerve to tell Robert Van de Castle that I was clearly seeing clouds of heavenly pink gently caressing his, from-all-my-experience, assuredly *pregnant*, lower abdomen?

My face flushed and once more I hesitated.

"Come on, Ray," Rex insisted. "Say whatever

you think you are seeing. You will not embarrass anyone here. All of us are looking at this with scientific objectivity."

I asked myself what I had gotten myself into, but tried to muster courage.

"So you're all scientific, are you?" I declared. "Well, then, tell me"—I blurted it out—"*how can Mister, Doctor, or whatever he is, Van de Castle BE PREGNANT?*"

I was absolutely shocked at Van de Castle's response. He didn't slap me!

"Fascinating! Ray," he said excitedly, "tell me more! What are you seeing?"

"Pregnant, pregnant, pregnant, I *guess!* Clouds of pink are so nestled around your lower abdomen that if you suddenly started talking in a feminine voice I'd swear to God you are at least five months pregnant. Honestly, I've never seen anything like it in my life—oh, I mean in a man, that is!

"If it is not too embarrassing," I continued, "would you please tell me what kind of weird something you are doing or have done that makes you have a pregnant aura? It's unbelievable."

"Ray," Van de Castle responded, "this is just fantastic."

"I'll say!" I kidded him. "But you're the one who's got some explaining to do."

"What I mean, Ray," the man explained, "is that what you have just told me is more fascinatingly evidential, it seems to me, than the personal things you said earlier. And they were rather evidential.

"You see," Van de Castle continued, "we asked Rex to be sure to tell you absolutely nothing about any of us. So you have no normal way of knowing this, but for quite some years my research, as a psychologist, has been into the content and nature of the dreams of pregnant women.

"Well, only moments before I left home tonight to come over here, I telephoned my colleague in pregnancy dream research and told him, 'You know, I've been working so hard to try and identify with Mrs. _____ in order to understand those dreams she's been having, that I'd swear I FEEL DOWNRIGHT PREGNANT TONIGHT!' "

A medical doctor (psychiatrist) broke into the conversation at that point to add emphasis.

"So you see, as far as I am concerned—and I probably speak for all of us—your telling Bob Van de Castle that his aura looks pregnant is so damned unlikely a thing for anyone—with or without ESP!—to say, and so natural a thing for any of us who know him and his work to *believe*, that I think we've already received more evidence of your using some form of ESP—call it auras if you like—than I had, quite frankly, ever expected to see demonstrated during the whole night here."

I could have closed the "informal test" upon that nice comment, but did not. Awarenesses about the auras of those present were coming to me fast and furious. I felt like the poker player who says, "When you're hot, you're hot."

With auras, however, success seems to me to depend about 50 per cent on seeing the colors and shapes around a person; 30 per cent on knowing what specific colors and forms usually mean; and 20 per cent on just that intuitive "tuning in" to perceive the meaning of auric phenomena never observed before.

In my "reading" of Van de Castle's aura, it was

only the tuning into *meanings* which had failed me, due perhaps to my shock in observing the totally unexpected. Oddly, however, it was for that very reason that the doctors found the demonstration so interesting.

If Van de Castle's aura was the most surprising one I have ever observed, it was by no means the most diversified or weirdly shaped aura ever encountered. Probably the best method, in fact, to introduce the subject of auras and the meanings of their highly varied colors and forms, is by the same way I learned about them—by experience.

In describing some of my more jarring, or, at least, fascinating aura experiences, it is only fair to point out that, speaking quite honestly, I do not know for a certainty whether auric phenomena are subjective or objective in nature. As this account of my experiences progresses, the reader who finds it necessary to classify the phenomenon should be better qualified to evaluate on a basis of the events described.

From an early age, colors had greatly interested and affected me. Yet, whether it was that fact that caused me to see auras, or whether seeing auras caused me to attach special significance to certain colors, I cannot assuredly say.

Yellow, for example, has always proved to be highly meaningful to me in knowing a great deal about the intellectual capacity and character of persons who were previously unknown to me.

Certainly I do not normally think of bow ties in association with women. Yet, on an evening in 1964 at a party in Phoenix, Arizona, where some four hundred persons were present, I could not help but be fascinated by the intense yellow aura that rayed out from both sides of the neck of a total stranger. It almost looked like a three-foot long, yellow bow tie.

The woman was in her thirties, and I am sure she became a bit self-conscious by my staring at her neck. For all I knew, she might have thought of me as a vampire contemplating her jugular vein. However, her aura showed no sign of fear.

I apologized for being obnoxious, explained the reason I found her neck (or, better said, its *aura*) so interesting, and added, "So, don't tell me anything about yourself. Just let me stare at those strange, bright yellow emanations from your voice-box area for a few moments, and I will try to tell you why your aura is so unusual."

Almost immediately, as I withdrew my attention inwardly in search of the sought-after meaning, pictures began to come into my mind.

First, I saw her at age seventeen, then at age twenty-two. Somehow I knew the exact ages, and "saw" her on a college campus "back East." Then I saw her before a music stand singing an operatic aria.

"I've got it!" I exclaimed to the now thoroughly puzzled woman. "Between ages seventeen and twenty-two you intensely used your intellect (yellow in the aura) to focus upon voice studies, with hope of developing a truly operatic voice. It seems to have been at a college back East. That's why the yellow, even now, after more than ten years, rays out of your voice box or larynx."

"It's unbelievable that you can get knowledge this way," the woman said, beginning to relax somewhat, "but everything you have told me is exactly accurate. Are you sure no one told you these things about me?"

"Answer for yourself," I replied. "Is it not true

that no one here except me and you could know *all* the facts I just related, including the specific ages of your intense study of voice?"

"Come to think of it, you're right! What else can you tell me?"

That question, and "Would you please read my aura, Mr. Stanford?" are so familiar that I am well jaded to them by now. Yet, if most any person could know all that the aura can tell me when I am really tuned into it and take time to "look" closely, the requests would become few and far between. It can be devastatingly revealing, even of one's deepest unspoken secrets. I more easily see the things one has either repressed or forgotten than those things one does not mind if I know.

Red is a color that literally sticks out of an aura like the proverbial sore thumb. Example best describes it.

During a fund-raising event in Scottsdale, Arizona, for a nonprofit organization, I was asked to let them sell tickets for aura readings by me. I agreed, realizing that I would not get any pay for helping out and hardly expecting the vast numbers of persons who would want my services.

The only condition I put onto the favor I was to do for the organization was that they sell no aura-reading ticket to anyone known to me. I wanted only the challenge of the unknown. What fun is there telling persons things they know you already know about them?

My first subject that night was a man of about forty-five who, for obvious reasons, will not be named. As he walked into the room I was alarmed at the red visible in his aura.

From the man's solar plexus and adrenal gland

areas, red seemed to permeate the interior of his body. Then it spilled out over his shoulders, down the arms, and flowed off his hands—especially the right one.

Before he was even seated, I saw an *auric* right fist clenched. His physical hand, of course, was not clenched—just the pseudo hand or "astral" hand of his aura. Instantly I saw the head and shoulders of someone intuitively identified as the man's wife appear before his face.

Wham! The red-inflamed astral fist swung up and slugged the wife.

Disgusted with what I saw, and being an outspoken person, I promptly asked the man to be seated, and after describing what I had just observed, lectured him not to continue such violence against his wife.

Thereupon the man confirmed that, in fact, within the hour prior to arrival at the fund-raising affair, he had become very angry and had slugged his wife. He seemed sobered by the obvious fact that his abuses of his spouse were no longer a family secret.

Additionally, red surrounded the same man's prostate. I advised he see a physician, lest the condition develop into a malignancy. He said he did not know whether or not he had any prostate trouble. Upon my questioning, he said that, yes, he had experienced considerable trouble of late in urinating and in the slowness thereof. I assured him that this tended to confirm my auric observations of an enlarged, inflamed prostate putting pressure on his urethra.

At my insistence, the man visited a doctor the next week and then informed me that my diagnosis had been very accurate.

The preceding account demonstrates the two normal meanings of red in the aura: anger and inflammation of tissue. With just a little experience, it is easy to tell which red is due to exclusively physical causes. One clue is the location of the emanation, but another significant factor is the *shape* of the red light coming from or surrounding the body.

Shapes, however, come under the heading of "thought forms" and are discussed in a subsequent chapter, for the forms that colors take can be far more diversified than the colors themselves.

The ways in which meanings of the more obscure auric colors—such as orange—were learned by me is worth sharing.

One evening in 1960 during a group meeting I noticed that a man in his thirties displayed an intense and highly localized orange or red-orange glow that seemed to emanate from his stomach, near the pylorus.

Ordinarily I would have taken such an emanation to mean the individual was suffering from an ulcer. What made me wonder was the deep orange color. An ulcer normally emanates red without any tint of orange.

Privately I told him of my observation and asked what it could mean.

"Well, I have an ulcer at the point where you see the orange instead of red. Could orange relate to pride?"

As it turned out, the situation of a boss constantly hurting the man's self-image and pride had contributed significantly to the ulcer. Thereafter I searched for any correlations between prideful attitudes and the presence of orange in auras.

A beautiful golden orange occasionally shows up in what I call the aura of a strong sense of well-being—even euphoria. The California poppy and the common cosmos flowers exemplify the most positive of orange colors seen in auras. Yet, such colors are among the rarest ones.

On one night in January 1957, I saw one of the most sordid auras ever encountered. A group of acquaintances gathered to discuss the forthcoming trip of several friends and I to Peru. A woman of about sixty was sitting across the room, externally appearing as calm and pleasant as could be. During that meeting her aura became "a sight for sore eyes," but one to make them even sorer.

Surrounding the woman from head to hips was an awful split-pea green. It was just as opaque and lumpy-looking as the famous soup. The yellow-green was literally punctuated with vile-looking spots of black and red, ranging in size from nearly invisible to maybe an inch or two across.

Upon noticing the unprecedented spectacle, I seemed to perceive a mind imbued with the most paranoid sort of unfounded suspicions, resentments, jealousy, and even malice.

Following the meeting a close friend took me aside and declared, "I had a weird experience tonight! I have never seen auras or taken them seriously. Yet, I suddenly looked over at Mrs. _____ and saw terrible-looking colors floating around her." The young man, of my own age, then described precisely the color and forms I had observed.

About six weeks later, upon returning from

Peru, I learned the actual basis of the woman's ugly aura.

I had just arrived at my parents' home when my mother mentioned the woman who had displayed the rather putrid aura.

"Mrs. _____ must be crazy," she said. "Just after you left I was contacted by the FBI. They told me that woman had called them and advised that they investigate your activities in Peru. The agent told me Mrs. _____ had told them she could not imagine why you and your friends would suddenly take off to Peru unless you were involved in some sort of communist conspiracy. They asked me if you had been reading any communist literature before you left, and I assured them you were not involved in any such interests or activities."

Thus, it would seem that Mrs. _____ had felt left out. She could have afforded the expense of a trip to Peru with us, but was not invited. Resultantly, some element of paranoia must have surfaced as a result of jealousy and envy of our not even considering her for our journey south of the equator. The call to the FBI was surely that elderly woman's form of revenge.

Her pea-green aura had appropriately brought to mind the old saying, *"Green* with envy!" The red was evidence of hostility, while black had revealed outright malice.

Over the years I have chanced to glimpse auras both apparently debased and nearly sublime, although not in the same person! In this book I shall describe not only those but a whole spectrum in between.

Then, with an understanding of the things seen and the conditions behind them, we should be at more of a vantage point to consider not only the question of whether anyone can learn to see auras, and if so, how, but to deal with the more basic questions that are bound to arise as we proceed.

2

Hovering Thoughts and Scrambled-egg Auras

Hovering above the head of the short, stocky woman sitting in front of me was a weird almond-shaped form that only slightly glowed. No, glow would be too positive a word. The form's surface looked more as though she had taken a shoeshine cloth and polished it. Color that form a pale scrambled-egg yellow, and you will have a pretty accurate idea of what I saw on that evening in Phoenix, Arizona.

Once more, I was benefiting a nonprofit organization by amusing total strangers with descriptions of things most people do not consciously see and yet which most everyone wants described to them.

I presumed it must have been a line of work which so bored the woman who sat in front of me, as to make her intellect, as reflected by the

lack of brilliance in the yellow of her aura, so un-
bright and jaded looking.

Without saying a word, I silently, telepathically, said to Ms. Weirdaura, "Please tell me,
what kind of work are you involved with that pro-
duces such a strong thought form?"

Immediately, I began to see fleeting images of
young people, seemingly aged from fourteen to
eighteen, appear at various places in the woman's
aura. Both girls and boys appeared. Some of them
looked unpleasant, or at least unhappy.

Then I noticed that each time a young person's
thought form popped up, there was a red anger
flash from the solar plexus of Ms. Weirdaura.

I was now sure I knew the profession of the
woman in front of me. After some moments of
careful consideration of how to say it without
hurting her feelings, I described what I had been
seeing. Then, I explained, "So, I'm going to say
you are a schoolteacher. But it bothers me that
when the young persons' thought forms are seen,
you seem to become uptight, annoyed, and even
mistrustful, almost as if you were calling them liars or cheaters. If you *are* a schoolteacher, my advice to you is start believing more in your
students. I cannot imagine why you never seem
to trust them. Now tell me, am I wrong or am I
right? Are you or aren't you a schoolteacher?"

The spunky-looking little woman just laughed
boldly in my face!

"Heaven knows I'm *not* a schoolteacher!"

"You're . . . you're not?" I exclaimed. "Then tell
me, what *are* you?"

Laughter again.

"You see, Mr. Stanford, I'm a TRUANT OF-
FICER!"

Again and again, aura seeing has provided an exciting learning experience for me. Yet, sometimes I tire of seeing people's physical and psychological conditions and secrets quite literally floating around them. Resultantly, I try to keep my noticing and interpretative attentions at a low level. But almost as soon as that has been achieved, someone will be seen who has such a strange, funny, or even frightening aura as to cause me to once more open my mind to its natural channels of intuitive perception.

In 1971 I visited the office of a businessman friend, only to find that he was out for the afternoon. Occupying the front desk was a tall, stout man perhaps forty years of age, whom I had never seen before. His aura really bothered me.

Returning home, the memory of the stranger's unpleasant aura kept coming to mind. There had been many red spikes raying from the solar plexus and mouth, meaning to me that he vented his anger readily by way of hostile words to others. Worse were the thought forms of only moderate yellow accompanied by some of dirty orange-browns, ugly greens, and spots of black that churned around his head but always flowed back upon themselves like some boiling cauldron of childhood self-pity, negative egotism, covetousness, and malice warmed over. Additional spikes of red flashed out periodically from the head-surrounding cloud just described.

So disturbing to me had been the stranger's aura that the next morning I promptly called my friend.

After describing the man who had been in the office, I told my friend, "Now I feel he is probably a business partner of yours; but without my asking you to confirm that, please let me tell you something. Whoever that man is, he is of exceedingly poor character. You or anyone else involved in business deals or partnerships with him could end up in serious legal troubles. I even have the feeling he could some day be indicted on some type of federal charges. There is vast self-deception in him, and he does not know how to conduct business honestly."

The businessman responded, "After that, I hate to admit it to you, as I *am* involved in some business with him—well, I might as well tell you. It's a really big thing, too. I just hope your psychic impressions were inaccurate. I think he's okay. So, don't worry."

For almost two and a half years I heard no more about the man or the business deal. Then, one day my business friend called.

"Ray, did you ever have anyone ask you to help them close the gate after most of the horses have escaped the barn?"

I somehow began to sense what was on my friend's mind.

"Listen, Ray. Do you remember calling me over two years ago and warning me about a man with a very bad aura you had seen in my office?

"Well, against your warning I got more and more deeply involved with him in a gigantic land development deal down in the Rio Grande Valley. Now—and I feel like a fool admitting it to you—it turns out that the funds taken from investors, which we had contractually agreed to place in a type of trust fund, have been absconded and squandered by the partner of whom you gave such dire warning! Thus, he and I have been indicted on various federal and state charges. I don't desire to go into details, but just want to tell you that if you get any impressions I should know, please call me, as well as keep me in your prayers. I'm going to need help. It was really foolish of me to get involved in this terrible mess. My entire career and reputation are in shambles, no matter how the charges are decided in court."

The court found my friend guilty of the federal charges, but because it was a sort of guilt by negligence and not by direct intent, he was given a probated sentence.

Seeing auras has proven to me that lies can be fairly easy to detect, if the observer stays alert to tiny details and changes in the auric emanations and thought forms of the person making a statement or claim.

Telltale auric signs of lies first became evident to me from carefully watching the head-area auras of repetitive, compulsive liars. Once the ways in which auric patterns consistent in such persons were learned and distinguished by their consistent absence in truthful persons known to me, I was able to look for similar telltale lie signs displayed temporarily by persons who do not normally lie but who do so on rare occasions.

Following a lecture of mine on UFOs in Washington, D.C., a nice-looking woman (had I not seen her aura!), about fifty years of age, approached me. Her head aura looked jittery as she stood awaiting my attention. She did not know it, but I had been watching her aura for several minutes before giving her a chance to speak.

"Mr. Stanford, I've wanted to talk to you for several years." Only a little tremor in both the medium yellow and also the colorless physical aura around her throat and mouth was evident at that time.

She continued: "Several years ago, in the mid-sixties, the late George Adamski, who had regular contact with friendly people from space, and I took a film of a domed scout ship right over my yard."

At this point tremendous auric tremors showed up around the woman's larynx, mouth, and cheeks—especially the left cheek.

She pulled out of her purse a still-print taken from a movie. There, dangling so close in front of the camera that all shadows were deep and dark, with the front rim of the disc entirely out of focus (too near the camera), was the poorest fake UFO model I had ever seen.

"This *beautiful* spacecraft," the woman dared continue, "just displayed itself for us to film."

At that point, the woman's facial aura was vibrating and trembling at a frantic rate. Some ugly brownish-green appeared around her face. Before she had even taken the photo from her purse, I recognized the aura of a compulsive liar. The "aura of a lie" might have been even more pronounced had the lie been told by someone who was not used to living a lie.

If the reader wishes for a similar lie-detection ability, I can presently give only a helpful hint in detecting chronic, compulsive liars—if, that is, you do not see auras.

The emotions that result from conflict about telling a lie are what cause the auric jitter around the throat, mouth, and cheeks. It is correlated with nerve and muscle tenseness. I have noticed that colorless tremor in the aura seems related to the nerves of the body, including those that control muscle motion in the face.

In many chronic liars you can notice an occasional jerk or twitch in a muscle located just beneath the cheekbones. For reasons beyond my competence to explain, in my observations such twitch has always occurred in the *left* cheek of compulsive liars. I have never observed it in the right cheek. So, although it is much more rare than the "liars' aura" and less reliable as a lie detector, look for a twitching cheek if you cannot see auras and suspect you are being told a tall tale.

Mention of the colorless portion of the aura brings to mind a learning experience I had in Phoenix in 1964.

Once more I was reading auras for my favorite "charity." A country-boy-type man was sitting in the chair in front of me. It was the variety of chair that has a woven cane bottom, with the front legs terminating in slight knobs on top. He had been there in the chair for at least half an hour, leaning it back on two legs, his feet dangling in the air. He was cool and casual about having his aura read.

After a while I noticed a type of aura I had never observed before. Along the inside of each of the man's thighs—all along them—there appeared tiny high-frequency waves of colorless vibration. Actually, I was reminded of the heat waves seen atop heaters, but the man's auric vibrations seemed much faster than the heater's, and horizontally about the thighs, not vertically.

Never having seen anything like it before, I was dumbfounded. Thus, I explained to the casual fellow just what I was seeing that so puzzled me.

"Shucks!" he said, chuckling, "that ain't no puzzle to *me*. See these here knobs in this chair? Well, they been pressing the inside of my legs [thighs] right *here* and *here*. You just been seein' my legs asleep and them nerves are just for the last ten minutes jangling like crazy!"

That incident, along with others experienced from time to time, causes me to feel that at least *part* of what I see and call the aura may have an objective, real existence quite outside the symbolizing capacities of my own unconscious. Yet still other auric observations, while revealing facts about a person, may be of a subjective, projective nature, related to the symbolizing tendency of the unconscious mind.

3

What Some Others Say

A more general description of just how the aura appears and what some others have said concerning it seems worthwhile.

Visualize the human body as a transparent mannequin that has the capability to transmit any color(s) from within itself, depending on how the "occupant" is thinking or feeling through that "body." Also imagine a slight mist around the light-emitting body, so raying colors can be easily seen.

In its primary and simplest form, the aura can be illustrated by such a magical mannequin. Any color or color combination would ray from it. For example, red streaming out from the tip of a finger after it has been pinched in a door would typify a pain reaction. If the mannequin tends to curse when angry, the red would often be seen to beam profusely out of the mouth. If it tends to strike the person at whom anger is expressed, you would know it by red raying from either the right or left hand (from both if it were ambidextrous).

I see the red even while it is still *within* the body (or mannequin) just as if the body were transparent.

If the mannequin goes to church and gets into a serene, lulled mood, its head begins to emit soft blue light. If it really gets inspired by the sermon, magenta might start coming from the mannequin's cranium. But it is rare, indeed, that people (or mannequins, for that matter) get so inspired merely by the words of another.

I can see it now: the latest Barbie doll, complete with a host of remote-controlled light sources and color filters. Press the blue inspiration button on Sunday (Saturday if you happen to be Jewish); the yellow-cranium button when Barbie has a bright idea; the pea-green when she is jealous; and never forget that optional button for the older kiddies—the reddish-pink lust button that softly illumines just the right spot at just the right time during a Friday night date.

To further illustrate the human aura, there could be a sex-education feature added to the Barbie doll. When the lust button is pressed and a part of Barbie glows red-pink, a flashing panel comes on which says: "Cool it, Barbie! YOU HAVEN'T TAKEN YOUR PILL!" When the pill button is pressed, tiny pink splotches of light appear at points all across Barbie's pulchritive plastic epidermis, illustrating the "protective," systemic distribution of certain "birth control" hormones throughout Barbie's body.

For less worldly children, there could be the Saint Barbtolomew doll. It would normally emit only white and magenta, but with the option of a nice blue when he is in a down mood. (The instructions could carefully explain that such a pretty auric blue would be an up mood for most persons, but a down mood for a saint.)

Actually, the human aura is not always as simple as mere raying light—at least in many adults. With age, responsibility, and attendant worries, "thought forms" (for lack of better description) indicating attachments, memories, fears, and hang-ups begin to be spawned in the aura, very much like clouds condensing out of a clear sky.

An aura seer can often deduce the source of meaning of an aura-obscuring thought form by its form and color. Thought-form colors are directly related to aura colors, and I shall describe definitive examples in a subsequent chapter. For now, let us take a look at what other persons have to say regarding the aura.

One well-known treatise, entitled *The Human Aura* by Walter J. Kilner (1965, University Books, Hyde Park, New York), claimed that the human aura as viewed by "clairvoyants" could be made visible to all by employing screens containing a chemical substance (dicyanin) in solution. Originally entitled *The Human Atmosphere* in 1911, and revised by 1920, that treatise, however, appears to have been steeped in naïveté and misinterpretation, if not actual pseudoscience. An entire volume could be written exposing Kilner's techniques and conclusions, but suffice it to say that the things "seen" by his dubious techniques have no resemblance to the magnificent colors and forms seen by me or by other psychics known to me.

Following Kilner's work was that of Oscar Bagnall, published in London as *The Origin and Properties of the Human Aura* in 1937, and republished in 1970 by University Books, New York. Perhaps the *republishing* of the Kilner and Bagnall volumes illustrates the great dearth of stimulating research or writing available on the human aura over the years. Bagnall's material, while interesting and sincere, fails to hold scientific water because of lack of experimental control and experimenter bias. Also, Bagnall's descriptions of aura types as related to personality variables correlate in no direct way with the real-life psychic perception of auras encountered by my colleagues and myself.

In a more recent time (1974) Doubleday Anchor Books has published an anthology of papers concerning Kirlian (high voltage) photography. Entitled *The Kirlian Aura,* and edited by Stanley Krippner and Daniel Rubin, the 208-page volume is replete with practical and theoretical data and illustrations. It even includes high-voltage radiation photography of a healer's finger in both "passive" and "healing" states. The actively "healing" finger *seems* to emit more Kirlian "aura" than the passive one. But recent research by Dale Simmons of the Toronto Society for Psychical Research failed to confirm any correlation between the "state" of a person and the Kirlian "aura." Such a result as an "active" aura may be merely artifactual. The results and discussions provided in *The Kirlian Aura* are, however, stimulating. They suggest that we may learn something about *artificial* high-energy fields by such exotic methods of photography. Yet, no evidence is presented to actually demonstrate that the *artifi-*

cially induced high-voltage field used in Kirlian photography and the resultant coronal effect obtained in the photos is anything more than a crude, *artificial* (due to applied high voltage) simulation of the aura.

Recently I contemplated the seeming lack of genuine scientific research on the subject of auras, per se. I examined the insubstantial efforts of Kilner and Bagnall, and reviewed the fact that the photographed Kirlian "aura" is obviously synthetic (induced by high voltage) and not a real or natural aura effect. Thus, I decided to ask a prominent and reputable parapsychologist what formal aura research has been done in *scientific* parapsychology. (There are plenty of pseudoscientific "parapyschologist" kooks at most metaphysical centers who will tell you that the aura is "proven." The experiments they cite, however, are very naïve.)

The parapsychologist easiest to reach was my identical twin brother, Rex, mentioned before. He now directs the new Center for Parapsychological Research in Austin, Texas. Dr. Stanford is a former president of the Parapsychological Association and is well-informed concerning past and present scientific studies in parapsychology. It will be recalled from Chapter 1 that Rex had set up the informal aura-reading tests for me.

I asked Rex about any *formal* aura research that had been done by qualified researchers, as well as for the overview of scientific parapsychology, today, concerning auras. He responded with some valuable information and insight which I think might even provide a valid explanation of at least some auric phenomena. Now I shall quote him.

In the first place, it is possible that the topic of "the aura" as an objective entity does not legitimately belong within the purview of parapsychology. Parapsychology is not a science which investigates just *any* claim or mystery, or even all claims as they apply to living organisms. Rather, it specifically and traditionally studies how organisms seem to respond to information about their environment which was not obtained through known senses (ESP) and how they seem to act upon that environment without known forms of motor (i.e., muscle-mediated) intervention (psychokinesis, or PK). Because a person ("psychic") who claims to have ESP or is known to have ESP also claims to "psychically" see a form of energy around organisms which is not currently recognized by science, does not put this claim specifically within the purview of parapsychology, any more than would a comparable claim about psychically "viewing" the functioning of the nucleus of an atom. Its most direct interest to parapsychology would be whether such a claim of extrasensory knowledge is objectively justified and thus provides more evidence of ESP. But that, of itself, would be of very minor interest from the purely parapsychological perspective, for we already know ESP exists and are not specifically concerned with whatever revelations a psychic through this means might make about other areas of potential scientific interest. We already know enough about psi phenomena to pretty much rule out the possibility that the energetics behind psi events as we have traditionally studied them could be the supposed radiating energy certain psychics—actually, a small minority—claim to see, for instance, around living things, and which they term "the aura."

Even if we were interested in whether there is any truth behind the claim to seeing an "aura," as evidence of a particular psychic's ESP ability, testing the truth of such a claim would be a dubious business at best! Contrary to popular opinion and pseudo-scientific mythology, it now seems clear that Kirlian photography has not proven the naturally occurring existence of any form of radiation around the human body, and thus could not in principle be revealing the objective existence of what some psychics claim is a radiating "aura" which surrounds organisms *not* being subjected to the electrical oscillations used in Kirlian photography.

So, it should be apparent why parapsychologists have not jumped upon a bandwagon to investigate the "aura." It is not an area which seems to fall within their legitimate purview.

On the other hand, one must recognize that there have never been sufficient investigations, parapsychological or otherwise, to establish whether "aura-viewing" psychics are really seeing anything objective at all, or if what is seen is *not* objective, what may be the nature of the hallucination, illusion, etc., involved. In this sense the questions of the "aura" has received little scientific attention, and to that extent is still a mystery and worthy of scientific study, if such claims capture one's fancy.

The only actual work I know of in this area is by Dr. A. R. G. Owen and some of his colleagues in Toronto, Ontario. Their findings suggest that a purely visual mechanism may underlie the purported "perception" of one specific type of phenomenon which can be experienced when attempting "aura vision."

As a student of sensory psychology, I feel sure that many of the things often reported as being "the aura" are nothing more than the result of prolonged staring at an object and then shifting one's vision, however slightly. Following this shift, one is likely to see afterimages which, if one is properly predisposed, can be interpreted as a psychic vision of the aura. Of course, there is nothing whatever mysterious about this to the student of normal human vision! Also, sometimes persons can stare so steadily at an object (if it covers a sufficient part of their visual field) that their perception of the image of that object begins to fade. I have known of self-proclaimed aura readers who asserted that this represents the becoming visible of the "living aura" in front of that object. Does one need to comment upon such a ridiculous interpretation?

Those who wish to see the brilliant blue "aura" of a bright yellow stone egg (which can usually be had in any gift shop) should place the egg on a white sheet of paper and stare at it fixedly for several minutes. Soon you will begin to see a beautiful, bright blue "aura" surrounding it. In fact, this is nothing more than a normal negative afterimage of the object itself, and one can further demonstrate this by shifting one's vision entirely away from the egg (but still on the sheet of paper) and seeing a blue "glob" appear there.

Such purely visual phenomena cannot explain the supposedly detailed, colored perceptions of "auric" phenomena reported by certain psychics. Psychics claiming to see such a detailed, colored, dynamic, moving "aura" are usually in my experience persons somehow involved with the visual arts as a profession or avocation. They are persons capable of strong visual imagining. My impression, based upon a number of careful interviews with such persons, is that what they see when they "see the aura" is purely imaginative in character. As parapsychologists well know, it is precisely such spontaneous, unrestrained flights of the imagination which can become a vehicle for the communication of extrasensory information to consciousness. This could explain any veridical content of such detailed aura vision and its interpretation by the psychic. I would go so far as to propose that some strong (vision-oriented) psychics use "aura vision" as a convenient psychological crutch or mechanism by which they can externalize the responsibility for what is essentially a delicate, internal mechanism (extrasensory response), and can thereby allow it to happen more spontaneously and uninhibitedly, without engaging the rational faculties which so often seem to interfere with ESP performance.

In short, for some psychics talented in the area of visual imagination, "aura vision" may be a convenient way for them to "package" and relate to psi-mediated information emerging into consciousness. Thus, their belief in "the aura" may be helpful to the use of their ESP ability. I wish to stress, however, that this is just one hypothesis about "aura vision" and its relationship, if any, to ESP. It is a hypothesis which has not been subjected to experimental test. It is simply one which has evolved from my considerable experience with aura-viewing psychics. It may be correct or incorrect. Scientifically speaking, we have not as yet fully come to grips with the phenomenon certain psychics term "aura vision."

Quite aside from scientific comments and theories, we may gain some humanistic insight by studying the experiences of those who, like myself, "see" auras and gain knowledge from them. A few fascinating books have been written over the years that might well be studied alongside my own highly personal and candid accounts in this present book.

If we take with a grain of salt the (to my mind, anyway) rather fantastic and untenable interpretations and explanations given by C. W. Leadbeater (1847–1934) of his personal experiences of seeing the human aura and thought forms, his books are otherwise very worthwhile.

In *Thought-Forms* by Annie Besant and Leadbeater (1961), The Theosophical Publishing

House, Adyar, India, and The Theosophical Press, Wheaton, Illinois), there are some engrossing accounts of thought forms, along with many fine color illustrations. The frontispiece is a chart of twenty-five blocks of color shades and combinations with a corresponding evaluation of the meaning of each auric color. Although Leadbeater differs slightly from my own experience in interpretation of subtleties in a few of the colors shown (or else the color printing is in error), by and large his color interpretations coincide with my experiences.

Man Visible and Invisible by Leadbeater (1969, The Theosophical Publishing House, Wheaton, Illinois) is a less satisfactory book. The same excellent color chart is included, but the thick Theosophic veneer that is intellectually imposed over the author's own intuitive perceptions of "man the invisible" are something of a put-off to those who prefer objectivity to occult dogma. Nevertheless, this book, also, is worth studying, but with due caution not to take Leadbeater's interpretations as gospel. The book's twenty-six color plates purportedly illustrating man's invisible aspects are rather nice, even if a little farfetched and poorly conceived.

The well-known American psychic Edgar Cayce (1876–1945) left as a final written testament of his extensive psychic experiences a little booklet (edited by Thomas Sugrue) titled simply, *Auras* (1945, A.R.E. Press, Virginia Beach, Virginia). The booklet is very straightforward. Judging by my experience it is a pretty reliable guide to the meaning of auric colors, although the verbal "color chart" on the final page is a bit misleading because of its oversimplification of color meanings. The book's thesis that certain planets and the sun relate to specific colors seems a bit overdrawn, at least in some of the correlations made.

Yet, if one wants a quick but meaningful understanding of the human aura, Cayce's account should not be overlooked. I do not know any reliable aura seer who would disagree with the basic substance of Cayce's account.

I leave this chapter with full awareness that neither Kilner nor Bagnall, neither parapsychology nor Kirlian photography, neither other experiential writers nor I have to date been able to say for sure what auras are or are not. Something more regarding the question of the nature(s) of the aura shall be dealt with in greater depth a bit later on. But if we are to ask qualifying questions about the phenomenon itself, one is justified in being curious, also, about the *reporter* of these admittedly rather bizarre observations.

That is where the person and personality of Ray Stanford must be discussed. Having been brought up with the axiom that it is not nice to talk about oneself, that topic shall be limited to the next chapter only, and to those facts important to the subject at hand. If you are more interested in auras than in me, great. But do not let that cause you to skip the next chapter, for you may get a vicarious look at *my* aura! It is no secret that I can see my own aura. But until now what I observe has been kept more silent than a butterfly in winter.

4

My Grandmother Is to Blame!

"Oh, Good Lord! I know Uncle Jimmie just passed on!" exclaimed my maternal grandmother as she looked out the window one night years ago in Golaid, Texas.

She explained to my mother that "a big ball of fire" had come down out of the sky and alighted on the roof of "Uncle Jimmie's" house about a quarter mile away. "Then I saw it take back off into the sky. Jimmie's gotta be dead 'cause that always means that the angel of death is takin' a soul back with it into heaven."

They ran down the dirt road and found "Uncle Jimmie" dead of an apparent coronary.

The "angel of death fireball" and, at times, "the departed soul in the form of a white dove that lights on my shoulder" reliably informed my grandmother Neilia of the death of close friends long before telegrams or phone calls gave the confirmation.

Whether Neilia's death-revealing visions were psychic realities, or projective visual symbols relaying her unconscious telepathic knowledge of friends' deaths, I do not know. Yet, if there is a physical, hereditary factor involved in psychic ability, I can always blame my grandmother for the unsolicited *psi* (a general term for all types of psychic phenomena) experiences I have had so abundantly, beginning in early childhood.

Hereditary or not, the potential for several types of psi phenomena seems to have been in-born into my nature from birth. While I believe that *all* persons manifest psi to some extent, con-sciously or unconsciously, it may be pertinent to mention a few of my own childhood experiences as a background to my seeing of the human aura.

I do not recall actually seeing an aura while a young child, but the things I later was to see clearly as light patterns were definitely *sensed*. Perhaps a better term would be *felt*. It is not easy to explain how I felt a person's feelings reach out to me or toward another person.

Even as a toddler I could feel when total strangers wanted to pick me up and hold me or hug me. When I did not like what I felt—when it seemed too saccharine or too "sticky"—I would try to toddle away into another room. Although my mother says I was a very friendly, smiling little child, I am sure she wondered why I often began a retreat just before someone asked to hold me.

It was terribly annoying not to be able to talk, because even as a pre-toddler I could understand almost every word I heard. Even rather abstract statements had meaning to me. Whether a past-life memory of the English language, telepathy, or a combination of both provided such an ability, I do not know for certain.

Once I grew up enough that my tongue could follow my thoughts, such psychic ability as I manifested became increasingly useful—even practical.

I will probably never know where I ever came up with such a pseudo-French expression as "the Foundier" (pronounced "foon-dee-ā") to describe my ability to find lost objects. Yet, every time a household object could not be found, the person searching for it would call me. Proceeding to a central place in the house or yard, I would throw my hands into the air exclaiming, "The Foundier will *find!*"

Rotating around like some 360° radar, while holding a concept of the appearance of the lost object in my mind, I would sense an almost magnetic pull in a specific direction. Knowing that to be the general direction the sought object, I would ask my mind, "Now give me a picture of *exactly* where it is." Seldom, from age five through nineteen, did the technique fail to work. The simple key to success seemed to be knowing the *exact appearance* of the lost object.

As I came to my twenty-first year, the ability to find lost objects proved less reliable, while other manifestations of psi function became more pronounced—all of them seemingly based on an interior *visual* awareness of something.

As early as ten or eleven I noticed that whenever I "saw" whitish-gray spots "within" someone's lungs, that person would later be diagnosed as having tuberculosis. It happened several times. In several other individuals I saw a purplish, grayish white around the heart area. Such persons always ended up having heart trouble.

I never called that the aura. It was just a visual sign to me about a person's health. I also experienced a "pulmonary depression" whenever I got around any person with tuberculosis. It felt—and still feels—very physical.

I was not yet fourteen when one day in an eighth-grade math class at Wynn Seale Junior High School in Corpus Christi, Texas, I happened to look up at my teacher, Mrs. White. With astonishment, I watched what resembled a time-lapse movie of Mrs. White getting very ill, then thinner and thinner due to a cancer that seemed to begin in the lung or breast. I knew, somehow, that what I saw was a few years in the future.

Throughout high school I asked junior high students from my neighborhood who were "back in Wynn Seale" whether Mrs. White had yet dropped out of teaching because of cancer. About the year of my graduation or soon afterward—I do not recall precisely when—students confirmed my vision of around four years earlier.

Thus, I was confronted early with the very heavy question of how much to tell a person of what is seen affecting their future or even present-time physical or psychological condition. I learned that there are no easy, pat answers, especially considering the fact that not everyone accepts psi phenomena. Also, people can be abysmally subjective about their own futures or health conditions. I learned that a person who takes even a doctor's advice with too much of a grain of salt was very unlikely to believe, "Some kid who claims to have X-ray vision—even into my *future!*" as one person described me.

Just why I should be so attuned with the physical conditions of persons often puzzled others, but it was never any mystery to me. *From birth* I had remembered living, just prior to this life, as a medical doctor named Clark who practiced medicine on State Street in Chicago. I had talked about having lived as Dr. Clark from an early age, stating that I had not been very much of a happy fellow. As Dr. Clark, I seemed to recall, I had smoked a pipe, been especially concerned about how immunity to diseases could be developed, had experienced much gastro-intestinal trouble, especially in the lower abdomen, and had died of complications resulting from surgery.

All those facts about Dr. Clark—except that he smoked a pipe—have now been confirmed by investigation via the records of the medical society in the area where the doctor practiced. There was no record that would confirm or deny the pipe "memory."

If indeed I was, as memory seems to indicate, Dr. Clark, he must have developed an ability to very accurately tell a person's body temperature merely by touch. By age six or seven I could tell a person's temperature accurate to one tenth of a degree by touch—even my own! I would call out, "You're one hundred two point six degrees," even before I was sure what "point six" really meant. It was just like some innate but remembered response—kind of like working a combination lock without consciously thinking of the numbers. I can still do it pretty accurately today, but not with the tenth-of-a-degree accuracy that came so naturally during childhood.

Quite aside from physical attunement with the physical body, by age thirteen or fourteen something more strange began to happen to me.

In conversations with friends or even strangers, when intense feelings about something were expressed by a person, I began, spontaneously, to see superimposed over that person a bodily form and clothing totally distinct from the present-day appearance. I began to interpret these as past-life self-image facsimilies, pushed upward by the person's unconscious in response to the topic or trend of the conversation.

I would not *try* to see them. It always happened spontaneously, even at the most surprising times. It is a phenomenon I still experience and which will be described in greater detail in a subsequent chapter. I am not even sure such experiences should be described as part of the "aura" of a person, since they may be a projection of my own mind, unconsciously devised to make "visible" to my conscious self the personality traits of a person which I perceive either by unconscious ESP or, at times, via unconsciously noticed "sensory cues."

It was not until February or March 1960 that I began to see what I call the human aura easily and continuously in all persons. I was twenty-one.

Thinking back on the circumstances, the fuller development of seeing auras must have been associated with my experience, at the time, of developing the ability to go into a meditation-induced unconscious state. From that state clairvoyant information was received and given for others to record, evaluate, and test. Such practices seem to have given me conscious access to my unconscious awarenesses, and hence to auric vision. Yet, it seemed completely natural—as if I had been seeing colors around persons all my life, but had just begun to *notice* them. Perhaps my occasional seeing of auras at earlier times contributed to the feeling.

As the months passed, a kaleidoscope of new experiences, of seeing things I had never hoped to see, was opened to me.

Gradually, strange forms and color combinations began to have specific meanings. Some meanings were intuitively grasped at the moment, and only verified later by questioning the person or his or her friends. With other observed phenomena, it took me months of aura watching and questioning to learn the meanings.

Although I saw in some persons' auras fascinating and even beautiful things, at other times I have seen very sad, disappointing, disturbing, and even ominous and awful things. Naturally, such perceptions can be very disconcerting.

Thus, after the newness had worn off, I tried to build the habit of not noticing auras unless there was special reason for knowing something about a person. That turned out to be a lot easier conceptualized than done.

For eighteen years (since 1960) I have worked as a professional psychic. For ten of those years (1960–67 and 1969–72) I gave personal readings, many of them medical in nature, done in co-operation with practicing physicians. Psychological and interpersonal situations were also effectively dealt with through applications of readings obtained through my unconscious state, called the "state of the readings." Throughout those years I also must have given hundreds of aura readings without making any charge for them—mainly out of interest in seeing how accurately I could interpret the auras of persons not known to me.

As of 1972 I ceased giving any personal readings from the unconscious state, choosing instead to use that ability in researching and probing the reach of my unconscious in giving information of use to science and to humanity at large. Much progress has been made on those areas, working with the Association for the Understanding of Man in Austin, Texas. Yet, I have also continued to read auras from time to time, under both rather formal and informal test conditions. It is the continuing challenge of trying to gain detailed, verifiable information, unavailable to me by normal sensory means, that keeps me occasionally reading persons' auras—to say nothing of what I notice privately and seldom discuss with the person observed or with others.

Yet, it would be well to mention my pet peeve regarding aura reading. Typically, a well-fed, middle- to upper-class, middle-aged woman is the peeve-providing party.

"Oooooh! Mr. Stanford! Of course, I don't want to *bother* you, but if it isn't too much trouble, could you please just take a moment to look at my *aura* and tell me what you see. It would mean so *very* much to me, you know . . ."

Such persons are usually accustomed to the phony flattery provided by "psychics" who know they cannot normally tell you anything significantly verifiable about yourself. Instead, they provide much mush about how spiritual you are: "You are an *old soul,* of course. *Very psychic yourself!* And, oh yes, your aura shows me—I can't see exactly *who* you were—but you were someone *very important in Atlantis!* I see a beautiful robe and a building with white Grecian-type columns. You are standing at the entrance. You have lots and lots of *spiritual blue* in your aura. Even *white*—that means *Christ consciousness,* of course!"

I usually refuse the request of such psychic-circus fans, or else warn them that what I see may not be very flattering—that I call them as I see them, and not necessarily as one might like.

Usually the lady blushes and says, "Oh well, I shouldn't bother you. I know you're a very, very busy person," and walks off. I feel most of us *know our own good points* all too well. It is often more therapeutic to have the finger put on the sore spot than to have our ego hot-air balloon inflated. To the best of my ability, I try to strengthen the psychological and spiritual legs of persons who encounter the work I do, rather than reinforce their psychological crutches.

From time to time I take a look at my own aura. Yes, it is even *visible in the mirror.* Having the ability to see the aura, even my own, does not necessarily improve my own emanations, any more than knowing that one is anemic helps that deficiency. Active transformation of consciousness is required to improve the aura. Just wishing for it to happen won't do it. Remember, the aura is an *effect,* not the cause, of one's state of consciousness.

From seeing my own aura—which, like most persons', varies almost constantly with thoughts and feelings—I must confess that it is neither a whole lot better nor a whole lot worse than the run-of-the-mill aura. It is a little more intense than many persons' auras; but, this means that when I become angry (for example) my red is more intense, too!

Hence, I have nothing to crow about, lest my aura become egotistically orange. My human weaknesses are about the same as anyone's.

I have seen many "psychics" and "spiritual teachers" running around giving instructions on spirituality, and even "how to become a master and enter the White Brotherhood, of which I am a member," while displaying auras that are among the most sordid and sickly I have ever seen. Because my own aura is imperfect, I do not insist that teachers have perfect auras, or we would have few teachers! But, I do think discernment about the teachers one chooses is warranted. I have noticed many times that a student of such a person often has a much nicer aura than the teacher. If for a moment such students could see auras, including their own, there would be a lot fewer such classes! Then, too, it might help the teachers to know the appearance of their own auras, or, by contrast, those of some of their students.

Along the same lines, I have encountered numerous persons teaching classes on "how to see the human aura." In most cases, simple tests have convinced me that most of these teachers do not themselves really see the aura. Pity their poor students. If they could see auras, they would not be so anxious to teach, knowing what a responsibility it places on the aura seer. But more on that subject when I describe false aura seeing in a subsequent chapter.

Until more is known about auric vision and the psychological and sociological influences of both bona fide and pseudo aura seeing upon the perceiver and even upon the perceived, it may be well that courses claiming to teach aura vision be curtailed, or at least be taken with a healthy grain of salt.

I have perceived much about persons that I could not have known by normal observation, simply by watching and tuning in on the meanings of auric colors and shapes. Yet, I am the first to confess that the nature of auric vision is not well understood. An all-encompassing explanation of the total phenomenon may be far from simple. My quandaries, experiences, and thoughts on this question are the subject of the next chapter.

5

Auras:
Objective or Projective?

A well-known parapsychologist whom I had never met before was urging me on. I had already been describing and interpreting his aura for about twenty minutes. "Come on," he insisted. "Is there anything more you can see that you haven't told me about myself?"

Indeed there was something more. I had seen it from the start, but did not care to embarrass him. Out of the scientist's anus sharp streaks of very intense red were raying out, looking like the streaks a cartoonist might draw coming out of some Sachmo's trumpet. With my own aura blushing, I described the scene to him, adding, "So, quite frankly, you have a *terrible* case of hemorrhoids!"

"Congratulations, Ray!" he responded. "You're *very* accurate. Last week the doctor told me that I must have hemorrhoid surgery very soon. Right now, they are very swollen and inflamed."

Within myself I must have grinned. Perhaps this was the first time in history that someone has actually *congratulated* another for telling him he had hemorrhoids! Maybe it should go down in the Guinness Book of World Records. (I guess auric vision does have some rewards.)

Sitting in the living room of a well-known Virginia psychiatrist, I was asked to read the aura of a lecturer from Ceylon named Frances Storey. This request had the element of challenge, which I always like, and since I had no prior knowledge of Storey's background or physical condition, I consented.

Immediately it was obvious that one of his thighs, both of which seemed to have the same size, length, mobility, etc., emanated far less aura than the other. (I refer here to a type of physical aura that is almost colorless, but resembles heat waves that seem to vibrate almost invisibly fast.)

After describing the puzzling scene to Storey, I asked, "So, is there any reason that should be the case? I do not recall noticing it in anyone before."

He smiled. "When I was much younger, I sustained a severe break in a bone in the particular thigh you have pointed out as 'aura deficient.' The bone at one location was so crushed that the doctors put an artificial section there. That would certainly explain why that part of the thigh radiates less life force. It is simply not alive, as is bone!"

Naturally, I was pleased at such a substantiation, and continued to examine Frances Storey's aura.

"Well," I continued, "I doubt you would have any knowledge that could ever confirm this, but I keep seeing a Chinese head and shoulders superimposed over your own." I went on and described a weird headgear, as well as clothing, and stated that I had a feeling this might be an unconsciously carried appearance from a former incarnation in China about seven hundred years ago.

"This is not surprising," Storey commented in a matter-of-fact voice. "Many years ago when I was traveling in China, two seers told me that I had been in the exact historic period you indicated. The outfit you have described is also the very type I would likely have worn in that time. What is more, a psychic of high repute in India independently told me the same thing. He even described the clothing you were seeing."

All this brings me to the central question of this chapter: Are auras objective emanations of some energy, or does the mind *unconsciously* tune in on facts about the person, or past of the person, and then project color symbols which the *conscious* mind can accept and interpret?

As to Frances Storey's one thigh emanating less "life force" than the other, it would seem that maybe I was genuinely perceiving some physical energy pattern. Could it have been a *heat* differential between the two thighs that I was contrasting, even though I was probably eighteen feet from him? Recently developed thermographic techniques of diagnosis might be utilized to check the plausibility of such an explanation.

The vision of the Chinese incarnation must surely have some other basis, however. Some persons have suggested that we each possess a second body of "more refined" matter which resembles the physical but is more subject to molding by thought. Believers in that idea may wonder whether unconscious memory could have at least temporarily reshaped that "astral body" into the appearance of a former physical body, with which the entity now called Frances Storey had been identified some seven hundred years ago.

It seems we would do well to proceed with caution in drawing any firm conclusions about such matters. The scientific method would be to take the explanation that best fits all the facts. Of course, all the facts are not known for sure. Reincarnation—much less the existence of an astral body—is not yet accepted by most as being scientifically proven.

Maybe we need not concern ourselves with the question of reincarnation. Instead, we can ask if it is possible that by telepathy I just picked up on what Storey, or others who had spoken to him, believed he had been (and even had worn) long ago. Then, my unconscious attunement with the Chinese idea could have been projected in visual images acceptable to, and interpretable by, my conscious mind.

Such an unconscious mechanism for bringing the telepathically detected data to awareness might have been necessary because the data was otherwise unacceptable to my conscious mind. Perhaps it was even too complex to have been accepted had it come in a more abstract or even a verbal form. I know from experience that I am what psychologists call a very visually oriented person.

Paintings, sculptures, and beautiful and colorful surroundings have much more meaning to me than, say, beautiful music. Yet Rex, my identical twin brother (who has seen an aura only once in his life), by contrast, appreciates art but prefers good music and even opera above visual stimuli. That is very evident by contrasting the interior of our homes. Thus, colorful, visual communications are very much in keeping with my personality preferences.

Could it be that my unconscious ESP is merely translated into a fancy "light show" to keep me consciously interested? I do not know the answer, but that may be a viable explanation, especially if one does not care for the idea that one's head and body are constantly radiating rather revealing colors!

What I next saw in Frances Storey's aura is a little more difficult to fit into a simplistic explanation.

As I gazed at his torso, one lung showed small cloudy-looking spots of a smoky grayish-blue coloration. It reminded me of the "cancer aura" I had seen in early stages of the dreaded disease, but the spots were small and displayed no red as cancer often does. I knew it was not tuberculosis, having detected that disease many times. I described what I saw to Storey and asked him if he knew anything that might account for it. (I preferred not to scare him by mentioning that it looked very like an early stage of lung cancer.)

He replied that as a young man he had tuberculosis, but had never experienced a recurrence. He said so far as he knew there was absolutely no trouble in the lungs. We left it at that.

About ten or eleven months later the psychiatrist at whose residence I had met Frances Storey got a letter from him back in Ceylon. Storey reported that he had just been diagnosed as having cancer of the same lung in which I had seen the small cloudy areas. Soon afterward, Frances Storey died of the disease. I regretted not having had the fortitude to tell him what I really felt the little cloudy spots might mean. Earlier diagnosis and surgery might have saved his life.

Is there a physical explanation for my very early diagnosis of Storey's lung cancer? Was cancer actually, physically, in the lung in December 1968, when I saw the auric cloud spots, ten or eleven months before the medical diagnosis? Or was the future somehow perceived by my unconscious and translated into a recognizable, visible warning?

Maybe such perceptions will never be fully understood or explained rationally. Then, again, there may be some simple *modus operandi* not yet comprehended, which could become accepted scientifically. Maybe the question of whether auric vision is an objective or a projective phenomenon is not important to some, when the phenomenon is sufficiently significant that a human life might be saved. But, quite personally, I would like to understand more of the *hows* involved.

It seems likely, based on my own experience, that some of the things I see in the aura have a basis in the actual perception (some of them through as yet undiscovered means) of emanated energies or even "psychic substances" such as the "astral matter" often evoked to explain such phenomena. *Other* experiences of auric perception seem, on the other hand, to be clearly "projected" as visions from my own unconscious perceptions.

One day while I was serving as a counselor at a summer camp for young people, another counselor came in from town with a fourteen-year-old girl who had just arrived by bus. The child was a total stranger to me, so when she asked if I could read her aura, I agreed. (I always prefer to be asked, *"Can* you read my aura?" rather than, *"Will* you . . ."* The former is a challenge, while the latter is a more believing request.)

As I began reading what I saw, various scenes flashed into view around her. The scenes actually looked as if they were in the space adjacent to her body. In each scene I saw a different young man handing her folding money as she was (in the visions—*not* at that moment) putting on her clothes. This could have only one meaning as far as I was concerned. I described the scenes and asked, "So now you know what I see. Is it true that, at only age fourteen, you frequently engage in prostitution?"

"Well, don't advertise it around *here,"* she replied. "But you're *right on!"*

While I wondered what trouble in the young girl's life would lead her to embark so early upon such a career, the space around her took on the appearance of a hallway in a house. She seemed to be filled with fear. Then a large, older man, who I somehow knew to be her father, came chasing down the hall after her. He held a gun. I could hear him shouting, "I'm gonna *kill* you!"

She said that exact scene had occurred several times in her home.

Such auric revelations surely result from a projective mechanism of the mind; they seem to be pictures of scenes psychically perceived in a perhaps more abstract way but translated into visual images. I sincerely doubt that the scenes described were really going on psychically, around the girl—even though they appeared that way to me.

Another child encountered at the camp presented an aura that may be a little more difficult to comprehend in the same context. It seems to suggest a rather complex interplay of unconscious phenomena.

The boy involved looked to be about eleven years of age. He had asked me to read his aura and tell "anything you see." Again, I did not know him, except for having seen him for a few days around the camp. I had never seen either of his parents.

As I watched the little boy's rather unusual aura, I continually observed the appearance of another person superimposed over it. It did not have the feeling of a past-life image, so I looked closely to see if I could note revealing details.

The man superimposed over the boy's aura was maybe twenty-five years older and perhaps two hundred pounds larger than the child. Then, I saw something in startling clarity. In the right shirt pocket of the man-image was a half-used pack of Tums (yes, "for your tummy")!

"Wait a minute!" I exclaimed. "Is your dad about twenty-five years older than you, and about two hundred pounds heavier than you, but otherwise looks just like you, and always carries a partially used pack of Tums in his right front shirt pocket?"

"That's preposterous! But it's *true!*" the boy declared. "It's preposterous you could know that by just looking at me—or even at my aura!"

In truth, the vision revealed to me that the boy had an exceptionally strong psychological identity with his father. I knew that he actually went around thinking, "Wow! I really look like my dad!" And he was proud of it, so much so that his unconscious even had itself "mocked up" as his father—right down to the last detail—Tums!

Psychological identity can be a powerful thing. I suspect that by now, twelve years later, the boy (now a young man) is beginning to experience the same chronic acid indigestion that his father obviously had. He probably uses the same antacid, too.

I think it likely that the boy's unconscious and not mine was actually projecting the big-man-with-Tums picture. But just how I came to perceive it as a visual image that appeared almost as real as "reality" to me, is another problem.

Some writers have held dearly to the idea that the aura, thought forms, etc., are totally objective phenomena, unconditioned by the perceiver. I am not equally sure, as should be obvious by now.

Several books on the human aura have claimed that the aura is egg-shaped and centered around the body in several rather distinct layers. In my experience, nothing could be further from the truth. Individual auras vary greatly in shape and change almost constantly. The few psychics who I believe *really* see the aura—such as Fred Kimball, Ingo Swann, and some others—all describe it as highly variable.

When a "psychic" tells me the aura is egg-shaped, I can know what books that person has been reading—without using any ESP at all. Persons claiming the aura is egg-shaped have never given me any impressive evidence that the aura they see can reveal anything significantly verifiable about the person being "read." Those who see it as highly mutable, on the other hand, *have*

given me ample evidence by obtaining information to which they did not have normal access.
But this still does not prove that the aura is an in-
dependent, objective, nonprojective phenomenon.
It simply could be that persons (psychics, if you
prefer) who can accept and confront randomness
(such as exemplified in the mutable-form aura)
are more psychic in nature and personality than
those who insist on *structured* living, and perhaps
as a result, believe the aura must be rather rigid
and egg-shaped. Recent parapsychological investigation tends to relate conscious psi function to
the less-structured life and personality.

Maybe there is an object lesson in this even for
the vast majority who do not consciously see auras: If our lives become too rigid and structured,
we block the flow of psi impressions and even
"guidance" from within our own knowing and
creative unconscious minds. If there is too much
structure, there is no room, no time, for inwardly
inspired change and even transformation of our
life situations.

While manifesting responsibility, that responsibility should not so bind us as to prevent our
minds and lives from hanging a little looser. Although we may not acknowledge the part of conscious and unconscious psi function in the daily
life, even a child can see that the wind does not
break the reeds that bend with it, while the rigid
limbs of the chinaberry tree snap easily because
they are very unyielding.

It is time that we begin to view psi as something integral to life and not as an abnormal ap-
pendage.

6

Auras Throughout Time

And it came to pass, when Moses came down from Mount Sinai with the two tablets of testimony in Moses' hand, when he came down from the mount, that Moses wist not that the skin of his face shone while he talked with him.

And when Aaron and all the children of Israel saw Moses, behold, *the skin of his face shone; and they were afraid to come nigh him.*

Exodus 34:29, 30*

If we are to believe the scriptures, Exodus 34 records the existence of an aura around Moses' face that was so intense it could be seen by "all the children of Israel." It seems the glow had an objective, physical existence, for the only way

---

* All biblical quotations are from the King James Version, italics are the author's.

Moses could keep the Israelites from being afraid of his glowing face is also recorded:

> And, the children of Israel saw the face of Moses, that the skin of Moses' face shone: *and Moses put the veil upon his face* . . .
>
> *Exodus* 34:35

Is such a *physical* glow from a human body possible? Biochemical research during the last twenty years clearly demonstrates that such a phenomenon can occur through the energizing of adenosine triphosphate (ATP) in the body. In fact, *during the last decade, three persons who have survived being struck by lightning are medically documented to have had a physical glow emitted by the body for periods varying from about an hour to over twenty-four hours!*

Could it be that at least a part of the human aura I and some other persons see is a more subtle counterpart of the ATP-emitted light, and that we are merely more sensitive and cognizant of it than most persons?

Be that as it may, the records of man throughout time are replete with both illustrated and written descriptions of the human aura.

As an example, more than forty references to the "countenance" of persons are contained in the Old and New Testaments combined. The best modern-day explanation I can find for "countenance" is "the light surrounding," or else "aura."

> And as he [Jesus] prayed, the fashion of his countenance was altered, *and his raiment was white and glistening.*
>
> *St. Luke* 9:29

Still another example of the use of "countenance" is:

... and his countenance was as the sun ...
Revelation 1:16

Chroniclers of the Inca civilization of Peru tell us that they had a word *Illa* ("e-ya") which translates as "the gleaming." It referred to the spiritual essence of a person, and they said that this essence appeared to human sight as gleaming light.

It is also interesting to note that in some parts of ancient Peru the "white God" Viracocha was nicknamed *Illa Ticsi*. According to Montesinor, this translates as "shining or gleaming base or fundamental of things." If the chronicler is right, then it would seem that persons of the Inca civilization considered the "gleaming" or spiritual auric essence to be a basic fundament of reality.

Hence, the Inca nickname (*Illa Ticsi*) for their bearded "white god" echoes an earlier statement of Jesus:

I am the light of the world.
St. John 8:12; 9:5

This continued reference to spiritual teachers in the context of *light* may have a deeper conscious or unconscious basis than a mere reference to "enlightenment." It seems possible that persons have always sensed, or even at times consciously seen, light around godly persons, saints, etc. Maybe the Incas were right. Perhaps persons who live close to the Inner Nature or God actually exude some "gleaming fundamental" essence.

People of the pre-Columbian culture that lived in the Muisca archaeological area located in the cold, high plateau of Cundinamarca, Colombia, produced gold figures by the lost-wax process. The largest and obviously most important of these gold figures depict humans with many expanding rays of gold seemingly being emitted from an *oval spot on the forehead* of the important person depicted. These personages wear distinctly different clothing from that shown in the more common gold figures representing more ordinary persons. The collection of the Museo del Oro of the Banco de la República in Bogotá, Colombia, includes several such figures. The rays expanding from the heads of the Muisca figures clearly do not represent feathered headgear. Strangely, one such figure carries, on each side, the *ankh* cross so familiar in ancient Egypt, where it was the hieroglyphic symbol for *life.* Do we have here, as among the Incas, some basic view of light as a fundamental life essence?

It is impossible for me to view the Muisca gold figures of the radiant personage without a deep conviction that the civilization that produced them accepted the aura as a fact of life.

The now well-known Dead Sea Scrolls were prepared by the Essenes (a Jewish sect) at the community of Qumran on the northwest side of the Dead Sea. It seems that they, too, were aware of a phenomenon wherein the face of a spiritually "enlightened" (unconscious knowledge of the aura may even be contained in that word) person takes on a glow, whether physical as in Moses, or more subtle. In one of the Essene scrolls from Qumran we read:

... Thou illumined the faces of full many ...
Psalms of Thanksgiving
IV, 5–40, ll. 111 and 112

Considering what the Essenes knew had happened to Moses at Sinai, it is unlikely this was merely a figure of speech. Yet, if it was just such, we must still ponder the conscious or unconscious origin of the phrase "illumined the faces."

From early Christian times, saintly persons have been represented in paintings and even in sculpture with halos near their heads. The earliest halos depict a series of lines radiating uniformly from the head. Only later is this reduced to a simple, elliptical ring of light. The specific artistic phenomenon of a golden, elliptical line, is almost exclusively the creation of Christian religious art. Art of other religions depicts their saintly persons with a more generalized glow around the top of the head, around the whole head, or even surrounding the entire body. I suspect that the elliptical halo, per se, had its origin as a *stylized* depiction of the intense head aura of saintly persons. It may have been developed to prevent obscuring the background of a painting, as might occur in depicting a more generalized glow. In other words, the halo is artistic shorthand that says, "This person is saintly, and therefore the head glows with a heavenly radiance." It is a symbolic representation of our old biblical friend "countenance."

From Oriental sources, many depictions of saintly persons, or "divine incarnations," as they are sometimes called in the East, are seen with auras illustrated.

An example in stone is the "sleeping Buddha"

of grotto 58 at Tun-huang. In this case the glow around the Buddha's head takes on a shape reminiscent of the petals of a flower—not of a lotus, but rounded at the tips. Beyond these are swirls resembling streamers of cloud that terminate equidistant from a point in the center of the forehead, as seen from the front. What results is remarkably like the highly stylized halos of the late Renaissance artists discussed earlier.

In ancient rock carvings from Africa to Australia—some of them tens of thousands of years old—lines radiating from the heads of prominently presented human figures are seen.

Throughout the recorded history of man—whether in stone, paint, or in writing—persons in responsible positions have recorded the existence of what the Inca people may have called the *Illa* ("the gleaming"), and what, for lack of better terminology, I refer to as the aura.

Why, then, do not more persons report seeing the aura in our present age? I have learned that many children *do* see light, color, and strange forms around people. But parents, fearing the unfamiliar, usually condition or threaten such awarenesses out of the conscious experience of the child. Yet, certain evidences have convinced me that, despite the suppression, not only children but *all persons unconsciously see the aura!* I shall now present the reasons behind my conviction.

7

Auric Eye of the Unconscious

It was Christmas eve. Listening to the choir sing carols, familiar since childhood, all the congregation seemed lulled into that peaceful, quiet joy so unique to Christmastime. Auric clouds of soft blue wafted across the heads of all of us, waxing and waning as the musical phrases of "Oh, Holy Night" ascended and receded. It was one of those magical evenings and all was well.

My friend Larry, the tenor soloist, exuded ebullient streams of golden and white-blue light from the top of his head, punctuated here and there with wisps of the radiant saffron color of self-assurance.

Then, without warning, Larry's voice cracked on a high note. I was watching the aura around Larry's head intently, and the change was drastic. The beautiful scene of a moment before collapsed into almost nothing, as if crushed by some invisible sledge hammer. Although I had not been watching the aura around the soloist's heart, just on the edge of my field of visual attention, I seemed to notice a brilliant red auric explosion, followed by a general devitalization of the whole aura.

Following the cantata, I asked Larry, "Did you almost have a heart attack just after your voice cracked?"

"No, I didn't," the tenor replied. "But the choir director almost gave me one.

"Only you would believe this," Larry continued. "But you know I told you I never had seen an aura. Well, tonight I *did!*

"Immediately after I cracked that high note, something fantastic happened. I actually saw a solid-looking spear of flaming red fire shoot right out of the choir director's face. It instantly shot toward me and *struck me squarely in the heart!* I actually felt it penetrate my body and maybe even my soul! It physically hurt!"

I was not surprised, having long felt that all persons perceive auras unconsciously. Only rarely is the phenomenon of sufficient intensity to reach the conscious level of most persons, as it did in Larry's experience.

Could it be that the meanings almost universally attributed to certain colors have a basis in seeing auric colors unconsciously?

For example, throughout the world the red traffic light is used to tell a driver to stop. Whenever I see red flare up in the aura around the head of a person I am talking to, I know there is danger there. I try to stop my trend of communication and seek to soothe the situation. Red was probably chosen in stop lights to suggest that there is real danger in proceeding; but why would red have that meaning, worldwide, unless there is a deeper, unconscious association?

The amber caution light is also well-chosen. As explained in an earlier chapter, yellows in the aura are usually associated with the status of the intellect. Deep thinkers have the deepest yellow auras. The amber caution light causes us to *think*—to remind ourselves to use *caution* if we proceed ahead.

When I see someone with a more intense yellow in the mental aura than I have seen in my own, I proceed with caution, as to the things I say and the way they are said. The brighter yellow means the person is more intelligent—yes, *brighter* (yellow)—than I am.

Green is most appropriate for the "proceed" light. The person with a pure, beautiful green in the aura (although exceedingly rare) is a natural healer and someone around whom you feel very relaxed. Green suggests, "Don't worry. Everything will be O.K." It serves to soothe, rather than to alert or instill fear into the unconscious mind, as do yellow and red respectively.

Of course, the use of red, amber, and green in traffic control lights is far from proof that all people see auras unconsciously. But there are other common uses of color symbolism supporting the same theory.

One day several years ago, I was sitting in a theater watching a movie. A rather attractive girl came in and sat down beside me. Soon, a soft red auric glow began to build up around her crotch. It was not long before that glow slithered across to my seat, up over my leg, and began to caress *my* crotch. Her hand soon followed.

I might have taken advantage of the situation had the girl's aura not also clearly showed the presence of venereal disease. But I will save describing *that* until my chapter on auric diagnosis.

My point here is that the soft red glow emanating from the girl's crotch gave evidence of the desire for sexual stimulation. It is not a wonder, then, that houses of ill repute often display a *red light* as a sign that they are open for business!

In Chapter 1 I described an experience wherein a woman's aura became literally green with envy. Further experiences have convinced me that other common figures of speech referring to color may have their origin in unconscious aura seeing. The continued use of such figures of speech suggest that all or most people find them highly appropriate. A few more examples should illustrate the point.

I have often marveled at the beautiful, soft pink aura that pervades the bodies of growing children. It seems that cell mitosis (division) may produce the pink auric glow in the growing child, even as it seems related to the rapidly developing embryo and fetus during pregnancy.

One day I noticed a neighborhood child who was at one of those stages of very rapid growth. As she played in the yard, the pink aura all around her body was much rosier than even the little girl's cheeks. I had heard the saying used many times, but it had never occurred to me why the term *in the pink* seems so very right.

While waiting to present a special lecture to a high school class recently, the teacher asked a tough question of the class. There was hesitation, then I noticed a bright yellow flash of light come on in one young man's aura. Within a second his hand flew up.

"Yes, Steve," the teacher said. *"You seemed to light up like a bulb at that question.* How about answering it for us?"

Did the teacher unconsciously see Steve's aura before his hand went up, just as I had consciously done? Her words suggest that she did.

In the very same context, what reader will deny having had, from time to time, a bright idea? Yellow has the visual appearance of being the brightest color of the spectrum.

In the aura, yellow equals *thought*. Do we sometimes give a second thought to a challenge and chicken out, turning *yellow?*—the source, perhaps, of one more figure of speech.

Over the years I have seen very few persons who display a genuinely golden auric color. Getting to know those rare persons has invariably revealed to me that they are selfless, loving, and true servants of God by way of service to their fellow humans. Knowing them, I cannot deny that each has *a heart of gold.* Could this commonly applied description of selfless, serving individuals also reveal unconscious auric vision?

By contrast, I was in the office of a business friend a few months ago. A colleague in business was trying to convince my friend to become a partner with him in a stock deal of some type. I became concerned, for the man's aura was profusely mottled with black spots and gray-orange-red clouds.

When the man of unwholesome aura left, I naturally questioned my friend as to whether or not he planned to go in on the deal with the man.

I was greatly relieved when my friend replied, "No, Ray. Somehow I just sensed that the fellow has *very dark motivations*."

Surely each of us has known or encountered similar types, and even used the same figure of speech to describe our feelings.

While still concerned with figures of speech, I might ask, "How often have we known someone who was consumed with a *purple passion?*"

Purple is a color that becomes prominent in the mental aura if one is consumed with the strong passion to attain a particular goal. That is particularly true if the person experiencing the passion feels the goal is a higher, impersonal one.

Have you ever asked a friend why he or she looks so *blue* today? When one feels "blue" there is a pervasive, very light blue, smoky auric haze that slowly churns around the head, and sometimes even over the entire body if the "blueness" is deeply felt. More than a figure of speech, blue is an auric fact for those who consciously see such things.

Recalling the choir director's reaction described in the beginning of this chapter, I wonder if any reader said to himself, "Well, that guy was just *inflamed* with anger!"

One day I got angry with my wife, Kitty-bo, and happened to see my fiery-red aura in the mirror. At that moment she declared, "Now there's no reason to get yourself all inflamed, Ray!" Coupled with what the mirror showed me, her comment threw water on my fire.

Again and again those colorful figures of

speech crop up in all languages and throughout the world. It is not mere accident, as I suspect some cartoonists know.

Have you ever noticed the radiating lines (in yellow if color is used) that cartoonists draw around the head of a person having a bright idea? How about the heavy red lines shown streaking out from the head or eyes of a person furious at another in the Sunday comics? Who would deny that they perfectly illustrate anger? Again, we must ask ourselves *why* it is so. I see the red streaks every day—not in the comics but in the auras of impatient drivers heading home on the freeway. It makes life exciting, but just a little frightening, too.

If the reader now agrees that maybe all humans see auras—at least unconsciously—then perhaps there can be agreement that it is probably a good thing that it does not come through to the conscious level in all people.

There are, after all, persons loose on the streets these days who are capable of killing just for kicks. How much more quickly would such persons react if they could see from your aura that you do not like their auras!

It is also quite a psychological burden to know by the auric colors when someone who you would like to think of as a friend is not telling you the truth, is hating you while displaying a smile, etc. Perhaps these are some of the reasons why auric awareness is suppressed to only an unconscious manifestation in most persons.

So far, however, I have talked for the most part of auric *colors*. Little has been said of the *forms in which those colors appear*. In their own way those forms are as revealing and awesome as some of the colors themselves.

Just in case you cannot see them, I next offer a vicarious look at the sundry and sometimes astonishing forms thoughts take.

8

The Forms Thoughts Take

A total stranger had called to ask if he could come and talk about "some odd things that have been happening to me." Normally I might have turned the man down, but because he sounded very sincere and levelheaded I gave him the address and an invitation to come see me at 9 A.M. the next day.

Promptly at the appointed time, the doorbell rang. Jim, as I shall call the man, was clean-cut, well-dressed, and polite. But the moment he walked in something about his aura astonished me.

Hovering over Jim's right shoulder was the human-looking image of a tall, dark-skinned, and handsome man of greatly authoritative presence. The mysterious figure had his arms crossed, much as a genie from Aladdin's lamp is often depicted, and wore a huge white turban with a gigantic ruby affixed to the front.

Despite the authority that seemed to radiate from the tall, turbaned figure, something bothered me about it.

Exercising care not to be too obvious in staring at a place in the air over the right shoulder of a total stranger, I continued to try and figure out just what was wrong with the displayed personage. I soon noticed that he never moved, but just hovered there looking important.

I also observed that instead of looking alive, like real flesh-and-blood, the appearance was more that of a paper doll figure cut out of some child's book. Suddenly the meaning came to me.

After about thirty minutes of talking about all the recent turns of events in the man's life, he told me a not-so-surprising story. I had not yet mentioned the turbaned figure.

"Ray, it may interest you to know that over the last two years three different psychics have told me that I have a great master from India who is my guardian. He follows me around hovering over my right shoulder!"

"And he is said to wear a large white turban with a ruby affixed to the front of it?" I interjected.

"Why, yes! Exactly! You must be seeing him too," Jim declared with obvious delight.

"Well," I asked, "what makes you believe the three psychics?"

"They all told me exactly the same thing that you did just now, and none knew of the others' statements. I think that's pretty good proof of the master's presence."

"I'm not so sure," I responded. "You see, the

turbaned figure that I see looks very two-dimensional, like a paper cutout. Let me describe a scene from your childhood, and you tell me if it really happened."

"Go on," Jim said, looking a little tense.

"Well, when I pondered why the figure over your right shoulder looks so like a cutout, I saw a childhood scene. Your mother is sitting on a bed to your left side. She is reading to you some children's story that has a drawing of a big, handsome man from India, wearing a very large, white turban with a jewel set in the front of it. He has a knowing smile and his arms are crossed like a genie from a lamp."

"Ray! That's amazing," he responded. "My mother did *often* read and reread that story to me over several years. But how does that explain my Indian master?"

"Well, Jim, isn't it true that your father wasn't usually at home?"

"Gosh, yes! My mother and he were divorced!"

"As it happened, Jim," I explained, "your mind was looking for some father-protector figure at that age. When you saw the drawing of the tall, handsome, turbaned Indian man with his arms crossed like Mr. Clean, ready for any task, your unconscious latched onto him. Everytime you have needed self-confidence since then, your memory has mocked up the turbaned man.

"While the other psychics took it to be a flesh-and-blood—or maybe I'd better say spirit-and-life—master, its two-dimensional nature revealed to me that it was just a remembered image, appearing almost exactly as was drawn in the book."

Jim was frank in his response. "Ray, I *know*

that you are right. But what bothers me now is that other persons could be similarly misled by psychics who see things but don't understand precisely what they are seeing."

I told Jim that a psychic should either learn to be very careful and to look very carefully at what is "seen," or else get out of the business and stay out. Further, I suggested that *all* persons should learn to use their God-given intuition, referred to in scripture (I Kings 19:12) as "a still small voice." If one is to listen to psychics, myself included, I told him, our pronouncements should be tested by that still small voice, not accepted blindly in a naïve desire to believe.

The three other psychics Jim talked to had been misled by the thought form I call the pseudo aura (false aura). Another and all-too frequent manifestation of the pseudo aura is the false former-incarnation aura.

Again and again I have known persons who, after being told some fanciful and often ego-building thing about a "former incarnation," have displayed in their auras mental facsimilies of the "person" the psychic described to them. In such cases, the projection looks no more alive or real than did Jim's "Indian master." To further complicate the matter, still other psychics who are untrained in discerning the pseudo aura from the real thing, seeing the imagined past-life image, "substantiate" the imaginary incarnation.

Most thought forms have a much more live, immediate quality to them than the false ones just described.

I recall several years ago, standing in a cafeteria line on a Sunday noon, trying to mind my own psychic business by not staring at people's auras. But hungry auras can be among the most aggressive of all.

The sign had advised those waiting in line to preview the food and decide what was desired, so as to take less time choosing when finally standing beside the food counter.

The first foods in view in the waiting line were those in the dessert section. At a mere 125 pounds I never have to worry about too many calories, so I was looking things over thoroughly.

I noticed, however, that a pale purplish, foggy essence seemed to be hazing my view of the strawberry and whipped cream pie. In fact, the rather ugly, somehow selfish-looking, purplish thing was actually *wrapping itself around* that strawberry pie!

Resembling some fat, foggy, gaseous, purplish boa constrictor, the six- to eight-inch-thick coils embraced the strawberry pie while the rest of the awful thing led back down the line, simultaneously cuddling a banana pudding, and fondling a piece of coconut cream pie!

Then, I noticed what it was connected to: A full fifteen feet back down the line, the foggy purple thought form was flowing like a waterfall of vaporous saliva from the mouth of a distinguished lady, well dressed in her Sunday best, who must have tipped the scales at over 280 pounds.

The meaning was obvious. The lady wanted the coconut cream pie, possibly the banana pudding, and even thought she might like the strawberry pie if the *one* piece left on the rack was still there when she arrived. The auric "snake coil" around the latter single piece was her own unconscious form of psychically guarding that remaining piece for herself.

As it happened, the woman took the coconut cream pie and then reached for the strawberry, too. Alas, as she approached the place where the strawberry pie was sitting, the man in front of her (probably unconsciously knowing he did God service) reached out and took that last piece— but not before the lady's passionately purple thought form actually *slapped his hand as he reached out for the pie!*

I thought it impossible to be more astonished, until the lady waddled back down the line and helped herself to the banana pudding, too.

It is amazing how food can evoke interesting thought forms in other circumstances.

One night my wife and I were having homemade Mexican food prior to a group meeting scheduled in our home. Richard, a college student, just happened to drop in forty-five minutes earlier than the scheduled meeting time, while we were still eating.

It looked to me as if Richard's aura showed signs of hunger. But when my wife invited him to partake of the eight remaining enchiladas, Richard responded, "No thanks. I'm just not hungry right now." He pulled out a chair and sat down with us, however.

Within a couple of minutes, Richard's aura began to expand in the general direction of the enchiladas. Moments later it extended a somewhat vaporous thought form that split into two auric tentacles began to reach out, around, and then completely embrace the enchilada platter.

Everytime I looked Richard's way, the embracing tentacles jumped back into the student's aura like some serpent retreating into a hole.

That went on for maybe five minutes, until I decided to have no more of it. "Richard, only minutes ago you stated you're not hungry," I said. "But your aura keeps reaching around those enchiladas. Why not just have some and get the hunger pangs and aura show over with."

He ate all eight!

I should add that almost the same thing that happened in Richard's aura occurs when a person has already had dessert and would like some more, but is too polite to request it. That might be called the "second helping" or "double portion" aura, and persons who display it at my house never have to *ask* for more.

In auras there is something I call the "withholding form." (It has nothing to do with the IRS.) This thought form occurs frequently, but a single description should suffice.

One day in late 1961, a friend and I were in the office of a wealthy San Francisco businessman, whom I shall call Mr. B, who decided to tell us of a rather wild scheme of his to financially help a group of persons who he deemed to be doing "spiritual work."

For maybe five minutes the man talked excitedly about how his scheme was proceeding. As the plot thickened, so did Mr. B's aura. During those few minutes, a bluish-gray thought form was building up all around the man's head. It had the shape of an Essene jar of the type in which the Dead Sea Scrolls were found at Qumran. The comparison is apt because the manner of the thought form's creation resembled the way a pot is formed on a potter's wheel. The blue-gray color probably was because Mr. B. viewed the project in a slightly religious way. But the color was really beside the point, for all along I had the feeling that one portion of Mr. B's mind was saying that he did not really want us to know the plan he was telling.

Then, as the man continued his description with seeming enthusiasm (the auric pot around his head having grown more solid with each sentence), a brilliant yellow flash from some level of Mr. B's intellect appeared above his head and struck the aura pot just like lightning. I could almost hear the crash.

At the instant of the "lightning strike," the pot-shaped thought form shattered into many pieces. The pot pieces hovered around Mr. B's head for only a moment and then began to shrivel and slowly fall like the pieces of a pinpricked balloon in some animated cartoon.

Obviously, thoughts *precede* words. *Only* moments after the "lightning strike" (the manifestation of unconscious rebellion against telling his plan to us)—and just after the pieces started falling—Mr. B lost his train of thought in the middle of the sentence and could not regain it. Mr. B. had been left with only those words that were generated in his mind *before* the unconscious withholding "charge" had built up enough potential to strike his thoughts dead in their tracks.

I could really not have cared less about what Mr. B was explaining, but the light show his aura provided was surely fascinating—one of the strongest withholding thought forms I have seen to date.

Sometimes I think the Incas were right—we

may have a "gleaming" *(Illa)* body that resembles the physical but is more readily influenced by thought. The difficulty is that I have no real hypothesis regarding what type of material would comprise such a body. Yet, since I have seen some things that make one inclined to believe in the *Illa,* I postulate that it is formed (regardless of the substance used) by thought. Hence, the *Illa* may be a very complex thought form, and one with which one often seems to be identified ("I am *this* body") during so-called "out of the [physical] body" experiences.

Having defined what some metaphysicians call the astral body, or *Illa* as a specialized thought form, I can now legitimately share a temporarily frightening experience my wife and I had one night about two years ago.

I still do not know what awakened me at 3:15 that morning, or for that matter, what caused me to look across the hall into our bathroom, about half of which was visible from where I lay.

In the illumination of a bathroom night light, I could clearly see someone I thought to be my wife, Kitty-bo, sitting on the toilet. (Who else would be using our toilet at 3:15 A.M.?)

I decided to roll over and go back to sleep, but what I next saw stopped me instantly: Kitty-bo was right there on the other side of our king-sized bed!

I looked back into the bathroom in alarm. "Good grief!" I thought to myself. "There's some *stranger* on our toilet!"

Quickly I shook my wife while trying to contain my mounting fear. "Kitty-bo! Kitty-bo, wake up," I whispered. "There's a person sitting on our toilet!"

My wife is not a sound sleeper. Almost anything awakens her. *But she would not wake up.*

I tried shaking her again. My whisper became a near shout as I frantically watched the person on the toilet lean forward and then *stand up!*

Moments which seemed as minutes continued to pass. Finally, Kitty-bo showed signs of life. She murmured, "I've gotta go to the toilet."

"Kitty-bo, listen," I whispered. "You *can't* go into the bathroom. There's someone in there. I just clearly saw someone use our toilet and then stand up and move into the shadow!"

"Ray, are you *sure?*" she asked sleepily. "I don't see anybody in there"—from her position she had a more complete view into the bathroom than I had—"but now I'm too scared to go in there at all!" She looked worried for a few moments and then added urgently, "But I've *gotta go.* I can't contain it much longer. I've never wanted to go so badly in my life!"

That settled it. I grabbed a brass candlestick from my bedstand and decided to go into the bathroom and take matters into my own hands (No prowler was going to break into my house and use the toilet without flushing it!)

I searched not only the bathroom but the entire house. No one was to be found. Not a sound was heard of anyone leaving.

Kitty-bo finally got up the nerve to go use the badly needed toilet. After finishing she asked, "Why did you just sit there in bed and watch that person on the toilet until he got through, and *then* wake me up?"

"But I just *couldn't* wake you," I declared. "Something was wrong. I can't imagine why I couldn't . . . oh, my God! I know who was using our toilet!"

"What? Who, Ray, *who*?"

"It was *you*, Kitty-bo. You!" I said, jubilant at my detective work.

I explained: "I didn't figure it out until I realized why you could not be awakened while the figure was on the toilet. Your physical body needed to pee so badly that you just got up from bed in your astral body—mistaking it in your sleep for the physical—and took an astral pee! You weren't in the physical at all until your astral body got through peeing and thought-transported itself instantly back to bed and to the physical counterpart. I was shaking your body when that happened, so *then* you woke up."

"My peeing astral ghost!" Kitty-bo declared with delight.

"We ought to send an account of this to 'Life in These United States' (*Readers Digest*). Do you think they would carry it?" Kitty-bo asked half in jest, half in 3:30 A.M. seriousness.

"Well, hardly," I replied. "Not unless they start asking for accounts of psychic experiences."

As chance would have it, a little more than a year later the *Digest* did begin soliciting articles on strange psychic experiences. But I never dared to submit the account.

While still on the subject of highly complex thought forms with which a person (or "entity," as I prefer) can be identified, I should describe something that happened to me in Phoenix, Arizona, years ago. When relating this series of happenings outside the context of auras and thought forms, I simply call it my favorite ghost story. Ghosts, as the reader might guess, are just highly animate thought forms—sometimes of the "living," sometimes of the "dead." This story involves a friend who was *both!*

Bret Stevenson, age thirteen, one of six children, accidentally shot himself through the brain with a .22-caliber rifle. He had been in a coma in the hospital for several weeks, and no one knew how long the body could stay alive in that state. His parents, knowing of psychic work, had requested any help I might offer to Bret, physically or psychically.

They figured it could be pretty traumatic psychologically for a spiritual being to suddenly find its body incapacitated. But the coma had gone on and on without death of the body, but with no improvement either, and this was pretty traumatic for the parents, I suspected.

One night before going to bed I saw a thought-form body of Bret sitting in the chair beside my bed. I knew I would have been called had Bret's body died, so my logical deduction and psychic feeling was that Bret was just projecting his awareness out of his physical body (which was at the hospital) and "mocking up" a thought-form body for a visit.

I think the reader will probably understand when I say that this friendly little visit "spooked" me a bit! (Who wants a ghost sitting beside your bed while you try to go to sleep?)

I shouted aloud at the ghost, "Bret, get out of here! I've got to get to sleep, and frankly, you spook me." The thought form did not budge from the chair, so I cut off the light and dove into bed, pulling the bedcovers up over my head in order to feel more separated from the specter sitting only a couple of feet away.

As I lay, head under covers, trying to convince myself that I could go to sleep, a singular and to this day unique thing happened. I could suddenly see through the covers, and to make matters worse, could see around the darkened room just as if it were lighted. While aware of objects and the walls, I could see *through* everything as well!

I had heard metaphysical jargon about "the opening of the third eye," but what I was experiencing seemed impossible—even ridiculous. I had been trying to sleep, but in that state it seemed that all the rest of my life I had been asleep through identification with the body, and now I was frighteningly awake in a way I had never, in my wildest daydreams, thought possible. Stranger still, closing my eyes did no good. I could "see" right through them.

The thought form of Bret, while formerly somewhat vague and cheese-clothy looking, was now as clearly perceived as if it were a physical body.

The boy's "body" appeared to be wearing street clothes, and there was no bullet wound in the forehead. I'm sure that was because Bret did not like to think of himself as wounded and in the hospital.

Surely I jumped noticeably as the ghost boy turned and spoke to me. I heard his words as clearly as any he'd ever spoken under less bizarre circumstances.

"Ray," Bret's thought form said gently, as if conscious of my startled reaction to all that was happening, "please don't go to sleep. Talk to me. You don't know how badly I need your help."

"But, I don't want to talk to a *ghost*," I declared with half-hearted conviction.

"Ray, I'm *not a ghost!*" Bret retorted. "I'm as alive as you are. And even my body is still alive back in the hospital. But I'm afraid it'll die tonight. That's why I need you to answer some questions for me right now."

I looked at my watch and said to Bret, sounding a bit irrational, but wanting to get some sleep that night, "If you're not a ghost, why don't you go talk with your mom and dad instead of me? It's 1:32 in the morning, and I'm sure they wouldn't approve of your keeping me up talking all night."

"But I already tried to get Mom and Dad to see and hear me, but they're not like you. They don't even know when I'm there. I even tried to pull Mom's toe while she was asleep, thinking if I woke her up while she was kind'a sleepy that then she might see and hear me. But that didn't work."

"Why didn't you try pulling your *dad's* toe, Bret?"

"I knew Dad would'a just kicked at me and gone on sleeping. Hey! You're just making up excuses, Ray. Can't you just talk to me for a little while about some important things I need to know?"

I had to admit that the ghost boy had winning ways and more than an ounce of persistence.

"O.K. You win," I told him. "I'll answer your questions for a little while. But your dad and mom will never believe this!"

"I think I can take care of *that*," Bret responded.

"I thought you said they couldn't see or hear you, so how would you manage to convince them that you were here talking with me?" I asked.

"I'll just tell you some things that they will

know would have had to come from me," he responded.

"That's pretty smart, Bret. So, what can you tell me to convince them?"

"Well . . . O.K. I've got it! Tell them I told you that since I have been leaving my physical body often, I've met a man who died recently and who my dad knew in business. His name was . . ."

"Wait, Bret," I interrupted. "Let me write the name down."

I reached for a pen and pad on my night stand, but something bothered me.

"Bret, I just thought better of it," I said. "I'm no spiritist, and am just not going to take dictation from any spirit!"

The thought-form's hand slammed my bed for emphasis, as the ghost-child's voice declared, "Ray, you know I'm not any *dictator,* and I'm not any spirit either, 'cause like I told you, I've still got a body back in the hospital. Couldn't you just take the man's name down to convince Mom and Dad?"

"Just *tell* me the name, Bret," I said. "I'm not good at names, but will try to remember it. That way, no one will accuse me of doing automatic writing. People around here don't approve of doing that, and I don't either."

"O.K., if you insist," Bret said. He seemed resigned to the situation.

He told me the name and then exclaimed, "Oh! Let me tell you how he looked."

At that moment a thought form of the deceased man's head and shoulders appeared hovering over my bed. It was as plain as a picture.

"Oh, I forgot," the ghost boy said, smiling.

"When I'm out of my body, it seems like if I think of something or someone real hard, I can make a picture of it!"

"So I see!"

He had done a pretty good job. "I'm an artist, as you know, Bret, and I'll bet that I could not have done as well even if I had the man right in this room and could paint him," I commented.

"Yeah. It looks just like him, if I do say so myself. But don't forget what he looks like, so you can use that to convince Mom and Dad."

I assured Bret while I often forget names, I never forget a face.

"Oh, I just thought of the best thing yet to convince Mom and Dad," the ghost's voice said. "I'll bet you think I was brought up right here in Arizona, don't you?"

"Who do you think you're kidding, Bret?" I asked. "I know you were brought up here."

"That's what I thought you thought, Ray," the ghost responded gleefully. "And that's just why what I'm gonna tell you will convince Mom and Dad. They have never told you any differently. You see, I was born and brought up in *Kansas*. That oughta convince them real well."

I told him it just might.

"Well, tell them *this*, too, and there'll be no doubt. Tell them that I told you that when I was just a little boy back in Kansas, my favorite thing to do was sit on the tractor for long hours and watch the wind blow golden waves across the fields of wheat. Nobody knows that but Mom and Dad and my two older brothers."

"O.K.," I said. "I'll tell them just what you told me. They should be convinced that you talked with me tonight."

On into the wee hours of the morning the ghost boy called Bret continued to talk with me, mainly asking questions about what he should do "after my body dies."

I answered as best I could, knowing that the entity called Bret was at one level very troubled about where to go. It was getting pretty boring "floating around the hospital watching operations, women having babies, and things." He even asked, "How do I go about getting a new body later on? I might decide that I'd like to be reborn somewhere."

Suddenly Bret's thought-form body looked shocked.

"Ray, my body just died back at the hospital!" the ghost voice exclaimed.

I looked at my watch, and then wrote on the pad on my bedstand, "Bret told me his body just died, and it is 5 A.M."

The ghost boy became more concerned than ever, for he seemed almost in tears when he said, "Ray, I have no place to go, and no body to go back to. I really don't know what to do. I can't talk to any of my old friends any more."

"Have you thought of praying, Bret?" I asked, "or maybe calling on Jesus to help you?"

"I don't *know* Jesus and haven't seen him since being able to go out of my body. So, how can I believe in him? I can't talk to someone I don't think I really believe for sure in. You're the only one I have found to really talk serious to. Can't you help me, Ray?"

The situation was a pathetic one. What was I to tell him that I had not already said in the nearly three hours and forty-five minutes that he had kept me awake answering questions?

"Bret," I declared, "all that I know how to say, I have already said. The night is nearly gone and I've had no sleep. Unlike you, I'm still identified with my physical body, and it requires sleep. I've never considered myself a really religious person, but I'm going to pray to God, Jesus, or whoever will hear me and act with positive concern. Now, please don't ask anything else. Just pray with me if you will, or I'll pray alone. Here goes."

I did not close my eyes to pray. It would not have done any good. I could see right through the eyelids.

"God, Jesus, whoever rules heaven and has spiritual dominion over all of us, please take, care for, and comfort this, your child, Bret . . ."

So desperate was I that it seems I may have shouted the prayer aloud. About where I got to the "your child" part, a strange thing happened. To explain it I guess it will be necessary to resort to metaphysical jargon, for lack of more explicit terminology. For, about that time, my "third eye" closed. The clear, distinct image of Bret became a vague, cheese-clothy looking thought form. The room now looked dark like any other room just before sunup. I never actually *heard* the ghost boy say another word.

Then an even stranger thing happened. I wish that my "third eye" had remained fully open in order that I might have seen it clearly, but it did not happen that way. Perhaps there is something so sacred about the thing we in ignorance call death that it is held secret and sacred until we ourselves must consciously walk through that "doorway" again at the termination of each incarnation.

Whatever, I wish it had been clearer to my

vision, but I shall describe all that I saw. (Somehow I know Bret saw it all very clearly and that it was good, for his thought-form body responded positively to it, as I will describe.)

Only moments after completing my prayer, as I sat there on the bed, three eight-foot tall, brilliant but cloudlike white, very elongated, oval light sources (psychically seen, I presume, though I cannot say for sure) floated downward into the room through the west wall.

As the mysteriously glowing forms drew nearer, the thought-form body of Bret seemed to float toward them. Bret's ghostly legs and phantom blue jeans seemed to extend right through the bed down to the floor. So did the lower third of the three glowing ellipses as they drew nearer to the ghost boy.

As Bret's three spiritual benefactors drew around him (right in the middle of my bed) I believe I said a mental good-by, feeling somehow that this was the last time I would ever really know him as Bret.

Although I may have imagined this part, it seemed that I also *felt* (not heard) a gentle, "Thanks, Ray."

The three elongated, heavenly forms, with the thought-form body of Bret between them, floated upward through the place where the west wall and ceiling join. I did not see them again, but somehow felt relief at having found some spiritual aid for Bret.

I lay back down on the bed at around 5:30, I believe; it may have been nearer to 6 A.M. I fell asleep immediately.

Forty-five minutes later the phone rang. I knew

it was Bret's father calling me to say Bret had died.

I picked up the phone. Without waiting for the party on the other end to speak, I said, "Hello, Mr. Stevenson. I know you are calling me to say that Bret's body died at exactly 5 A.M. this morning. Aren't you?"

"Ray! How did you know? You're the first person I've called because I knew you had a genuine spiritual concern for Bret," Mr. Stevenson said.

"I know because Bret was in my bedroom talking and asking questions about life after death all night."

He asked me to come over and to tell him and his wife what had happened in detail. If the experience proved convincing to them, he wanted me to then tell it to the five remaining children. Naturally, I immediately went to the Stevensons' home, despite the lack of sleep.

When I came to the part about the business acquaintance of Mr. Stevenson's, whom Bret had named and of whom he had projected a thought-form picture, I could not recall the name (having refused to "take dictation" from a "ghost"), but both Bret's father and mother immediately recognized the man from my description of Bret's projected image.

When I got to the part about Bret telling me of his having been brought up in Kansas and how his favorite pastime was sitting on the tractor watching the wind blow waves across the golden fields of wheat, both were totally convinced that I had really talked with Bret in his thought-form body, as were the five children when they later came in to hear my account.

A few days later at Bret's funeral, the Stevensons' kinfolk, religious fundamentalists who had come in from Kansas for the occasion, shed "crocodile tears," but Bret's parents and the five children sat in the front pew with dry eyes and occasionally even smiles.

Afterward, one of the outraged kinfolk complained, "I never thought I'd see any good Christians sit at their own child's funeral and *not cry*. You have fallen under the influence of Satan! Any good Christian knows death is a sorrowful thing and would cry at the death of a son. Don't you know Bret is DEAD? You should repent of your pagan beliefs and *be saved*."

Mrs. Stevenson responded, "Quite frankly, I think it is more Christian to know that Bret still lives, spiritually, and that life is eternal, as Jesus promised us. *Our* Christianity is one of joy, not of doubtful weeping. We know Bret lives and is in good hands."

I have seen some thought forms emanating from *incarnate* entities which were much more unpleasant than any ghost I have ever encountered. One type is that produced by the jealous person described earlier, which appears as ugly pea-green, and is often covered with black (malice) spots surrounded by red. But I have not yet described the awful thought forms that often extend out *from* the ugly auras of such jealous persons. Those forms frequently resemble big, flexible meat hooks. Color them fiery red with black in the inside. Such forms reach out and actually *claw* at the person envied, as if trying to tear that one's eyes out or head off; or, in some bizarre cases, if the person has sexually rejected the jealous one and become involved with another, the black-and-red auric claws and grappling hooks actually seem to be trying to claw the sexual organs off of, or out of, the offender's body! The latter manifestation is generated by the type of person who becomes insanely jealous.

There are persons from whom the meat hook aura exudes (in diverse sizes and color intensities) nearly all the time. Such persons are usually beyond any immediate help. I try to avoid them, since they usually leech one's energy, if nothing worse. Such persons are always very selfish and libidinous.

Another unpleasant type of thought form is exemplified by one I saw during a lecture recently. A nice-looking young man was sitting in the front row attentively listening to my talk. Something near him attracted my attention: an ugly reddish-purple cloud of thought-form substance (whatever that is!) was building up on or just above the young man's lap! I could hardly believe my eyes, for it was not characteristic of the colors or forms I would have expected anyone so decent-looking to exude.

Puzzled, I glanced occasionally at the ugly, cloudy mass reposing on the youth's lap. I noticed that it began to move sneakily down around the crotch; and then, to my astonishment, it began to slowly vibrate while seemingly fondling his "privates."

Although I hoped my lecture was not so boring as to allow an active, youthful mind to wander, the thought form made me curious as to whether the person involved was engaging in some type of mental masturbation.

It was not until I moved to the chalkboard at the other side of the room that I noticed who was behind the youth. Sitting directly behind him was a lecherous-looking middle-aged male of effeminate appearance. From the man's right hand (which rested on his own thigh) a cloudy, reddish-purple tube of highly sensual thought form exuded under the youth's chair, through the seat of the chair, and up between the youth's legs, where it was doing its thing! (Or should I say the youth's?)

Sometimes I wonder whether if everyone could see everyone else's auras and thought forms, they would control their thoughts and imaginations a bit more carefully.

Many times I have noticed a type of rather nice thought form that no one need conceal. It seems to predominate in certain women, and very rarely in men. I believe the figure of speech "bubbly," as in, "You know, she has such a delightful, *bubbly*, joy-of-life personality," has its origins in the type of thought form to which I refer.

In this case, the type of woman who is very womanly, but not "earthy," the type who says she is "really glad to be a woman" (not the "women's lib" type), often displays, coming out of one or both eyes, *bubbles that rise upward and expand like the bubbles in a carbonated beverage!* The color of the bubbles depends upon the personality or mood. They can be a nice blue, yellow, or whitish.

Sometimes the bubbles pop out of the eye slowly, sometimes they just stream out. I call the latter the *champagne aura*. But once when without prior explanation I referred to one woman's "champagne aura," she defensively declared, "Mr. Stanford, I'm *not* an alcoholic, if that's what you're implying!"

Perhaps the most unique thought forms I have

ever seen occurred around metallic objects that were about to bend or break under the influence of Uri Geller—*even when he was over a thousand miles away from the object involved.*

Because Geller is not the subject of this book, I shall not describe the well-documented occurrences of metal bending, breaking, and, in one case, even *slowly dissolving,* before the eyes of my wife and me, which occurred in association with him. Some of these events involved objects Geller had neither seen, nor even been near to, which were altered in Austin, Texas, my present home, *after* he had gone back to New York.

Suffice it to say that in every case of directly observed "Gellerization," as I have come to call it, a metallic-looking, blue-white glow has formed around each object within a minute or so before it altered.

When Geller is present, the strange metallic glow also forms around the arm and hand he is holding on or near the object which is to be altered. Sometimes it forms as concentric spheres that increase in brightness and diameter until the object which the light surrounds completes bending or breaking. This also occurred in the case of a silver cross and its stone base which *slowly dissolved* before our eyes.

I have never seen a blue-whitish metallic glow around or associated with any human being other than Uri Geller. Therefore, since the experience is unprecedented, I do not know what the metallic-looking aura may mean, except that it is associated with the paranormal alteration of objects.

"Does this mean Uri could be an *extraterrestrial* entity incarnate in a human body?" one person asked me. Well, the rest of Uri's aura looks very human, although it is much more powerful and intense than most persons' auras. Frankly, I do not know how to interpret what is seen there, but would discourage jumping to any extreme conclusions.

The mysterious manifestation in Geller's aura came as a real surprise to me, even though I should have anticipated a somewhat unusual array of auric energy. But then, auras and thought forms have a way of revealing the unexpected. That is true even as to what the aura can show, at times, about the occupation, past activities, or repressed memories of a person. The aura even tells me things, at times, about animals. In the next chapter we take a look at all these.

9

The Naked Truth

No matter how fancy the clothes, how thick the make-up, or how well guarded one's true feelings are, a person cannot normally keep the real and hidden side of oneself from anyone experienced and alert in reading the aura. The naked truth is always there to see.

In fact, the more one disbelieves in my ability to see the aura, or the more one is afraid of what I might see (most persons who disbelieve really just seem to be afraid of the implications of accepting auric vision), *the more easily I can see that person's hidden side!* To psychologists and parapsychologists I leave the problem of determining why that is the case. For me, it is just a practical matter of having fun with skeptics who would like to make a fool out of me.

Sometimes when I am on a lecture tour, a husband will say something like, "My wife wanted to meet you, but she stayed home, afraid of what you would see." (This has happened often.)

"That's pathetic, because I probably wouldn't see anything all too different from something I've already seen somewhere else," I typically answer. "In fact, I try not to notice unless something is really odd, or unless something catches my eye that I feel one should know about. After all, tell your wife my judgment of her would probably not be as severe as that of her own inner consciousness. Since it is herself and you she has to live with, not *me*, she shouldn't give it a second thought."

When I pay much attention to auras, it is just for fun and games. Knowing some of people's personal secrets gets old after a while. Then, too, aura viewing is not like reading one's conscious thoughts; it is more like reading one's *feelings*, desires, past experiences, and physical conditions. Of course, I sometimes pick up direct thoughts, words, and even numbers, but that is not usually done by aura reading.

Before a person is going to die, even unexpectedly or by "accident," the aura seems to withdraw, leaving the person without much, or any, auric light. That is very noticeable when one is used to seeing auras around everyone.

The same thing happens with animals, although their auras are usually not as complex, colorful, or mutable as the human aura. This is exemplified in what happened with a large fish, an arowana (*Osteoglossum bicirrhosum*), that I kept in an aquarium in Phoenix.

One night I repeatedly noticed that the aura of the arowana was dark or drawn within the body of the fish. That had never happened before.

Knowing that the fish had the unfortunate habit of sometimes jumping up during the night and hitting the metal light cabinet atop the aquarium, I felt the withdrawn, predeath-type aura suggested that the fish would probably kill itself that night by hitting the metal too hard.

Because of what I saw and its probable meaning, I tried to send the fish some soothing, telepathic messages and attempted to "hold it in the light" mentally, which can sometimes serve to reignite an extinguished aura.

I went to bed around 11 P.M. About 2 A.M. the loudest crash I have ever heard from an aquarium awakened me.

The eighteen-inch fish had knocked itself unconscious on the metal atop the aquarium. The arowana did not seem to be pumping water through its gills, so I gave it artificial respiration. (Thank heavens it did not require mouth-to-mouth resuscitation!) The fish survived, but I wondered if it would have, had I not also artificially revitalized its aura earlier. Skeptics will say it was all the artificial respiration that helped, but I think the accident would have been more serious if I had not earlier shared a bit of my own auric energy with that beautiful aquatic descendent of the Jurassic Age. The fish had never shown itself as auraless before, and it never did again as long as I had it. I traded it for smaller fish after a few months. That was the only night it ever knocked itself unconscious.

I used to play a game with a pair of mature fresh-water angelfish when they had eggs laid in a plant leaf. I would put my hand into the water and approach the eggs. The angry fish would turn sideways and attack my hand, biting it furiously.

It was worth the little nip to see how marvelously red their auras flared up. Surely psychologists will say this was only an inherited reaction; that fish have no emotions. I know better than that. No creature could display such an intense aura without being *very angry*. Since in the aquarium the angelfish had no natural enemies from which to protect the eggs, my little game probably helped them stay healthy and emotionally fit. (That is how I justified it, anyway.)

On one occasion, red in the human aura told me something unusual and additional to what it normally reveals.

On that evening I was giving a talk and aura-reading demonstration to members of a spiritist church. I had been a little apprehensive about accepting the invitation to speak because I generally do not approve of spiritism, on philosophical grounds. But the minister told me he would be out of town and badly needed a speaker for that Wednesday evening, so I agreed.

During the aura-reading and question period, someone asked, "Can you tell just by looking at the auras of those present which persons are either spirit mediums or are developing mediumship?"

"That's quite a challenge, because your auras blend together with you sitting so near each other," I replied. "But, I will try."

Quickly I scanned the audience of about 150 persons row-by-row, looking for the normal signs of mediumistic tendencies: a thought-form person or persons hovering within the aura. Sometimes that image of a person seems to be from an outside entity. At other times it is merely the imagining of the person who thinks of himself or herself as a medium. Either way, it usually indicates that the person in whose aura it appears has mediumistic tendencies or desires.

By the time I had finished scanning the audience, I had pointed out eleven persons as having mediumistic auras. The regular church members were very much impressed, because out of twelve mediums and mediumship trainees in the church, I had picked eleven of them out of an audience of strangers. Furthermore, I had not pointed out anyone who was not the type for which I was looking.

One of the eleven persons was chosen by me because I saw the thought form of a "spirit" with a very bad aura hovering behind the man seemingly attracted to one of his dorsal vertebrae—the twelfth dorsal, if I recall accurately—from which red light was raying. The "entity" seemed to literally be absorbing the outflowing red light.

Somehow I knew that the red light was due to nerve irritation in the area of the back which it surrounded, and knew the man must have sustained a rather painful injury to that region.

When I told the man about the red emanation and what I felt about it, he responded, "You're very accurate. About three months ago I was trying a fancy dive from a diving board, but my back hit the end of the board at precisely where you pointed. I've had great pain there ever since. I keep wanting to see a doctor but put off making an appointment."

I did not have the nerve to say, in front of all these spiritists, that there was a lower-order thought-form "spirit" leeching energy from the man's injury. Instead I asked, "Isn't it true that recently you have felt as if the energy were being drained from your physical body?"

"Exactly!" he declared. "But how can you tell that?" (He was the healthy-looking, very muscular type.)

Not wanting to say anything about how lower spirits can misuse persons (for fear of angering the spiritists), I only replied, "Well, you're losing so much energy through those red sore-back emanations that I don't see how you could have much energy left. If you get proper treatment, your energy level will return to normal."

Later the same evening, something kept bothering me as I was reading the aura of another man who was standing to my right on the stage. From my left—the direction of the audience—I kept noticing a cloudy, light bluish shaft reaching out and attaching itself to the aura of the man I was reading. I became annoyed with the strange phenomenon and turned slowly around, visually following it back to its source in the audience. The shaft came from a man sitting in the far back of the room.

"Hey, you," I said, pointing at the man, who I hoped would not be offended. "Quit distracting me by reading this man's aura while I am doing so!" (The audience laughed.) Then I described what I had seen.

The man in the audience stood up. In his thick red-and-black-plaid shirt, he looked more like Paul Bunyan than a "psychic personality."

"I've got to confess something!" he shouted.

"I'm not a priest," I responded jokingly.

"Well, I'm not a confessor, either. Maybe I should have asked to *testify*."

"Tell it like it is!" I said.

"Well, I have secretly seen auras for many years. Never even told my wife. As you were reading the aura just now, I felt very guilty reading it along with you, and I'll have to admit that I felt I was creating some sort of 'awareness tube' connecting myself with his aura. So, you're right on in what you described."

"Then, since you see auras, too, why not tell me something about mine?" I challenged. "Let's not let this be a one-sided thing."

"O.K.," the man replied, shouting again so everyone could hear him. "I've been wondering about the red-headed girl in a kind of greenish Ban-lon shirt. I've seen her hovering over your right shoulder all evening."

"Oh, heck!" I said, grinning. "How did she manage to get out of my wallet?" Then I went on to open my wallet and reveal a color photo of a red-headed girl in a greenish Ban-lon shirt.

The man ran up and looked at the picture, "Yep! That's the girl I saw."

I explained that only that morning the photo had arrived by mail from a girl in Sweden with whom I was corresponding. (The girl later came to the United States and married my twin brother, Rex.)

Birgit, the girl in the photo, had not been on my conscious mind at all. He must have perceived her in my unconscious, as is usually the case in psychic awareness.

This matter of carrying a friend in the aura (or in the unconscious mind) brings to my memory the frequent occasions when I have seen a person's job in his or her aura.

I know many people like to think they leave the office behind at 5 P.M. That is, however, the very type of person who is likely to carry it along all the time.

One day I was wondering why the aura of a total stranger was so dull and uninspired looking. I telepathically asked him to display his work to me, as I somehow felt that to be the cause of the dull-colored yellow I saw.

Momentarily, I saw "behind" him what looked like a wall of small boxes into which he seemed to be sorting something that looked like letters. I could not resist asking the man, "Do you work in the post office?"

"Yes," he said. "But how do you know? I never work behind the front counter."

When I explained that "I simply saw it around you," he looked as puzzled as I sometimes do when it takes a letter a week to reach me from a city eighty miles away.

One day fifteen years ago, I saw a man in a business suit come aboard an airliner and seat himself in the same row I was in, but across the aisle. In the man's aura I saw a stethoscope hanging from his neck.

That had to mean he was a medical doctor, so I asked the little old lady beside me to call across the aisle and verify my perception.

"Why *yes*, I am!" the doctor replied. "Would you please ask the young man if he knows me and, if not, how he knew?"

When the lady relayed word that I knew just because everytime I looked at him I saw a stethoscope around his neck, the doctor told the lady, "Well, I don't know the young man either, but he certainly has an amazing ability!"

That surprised me, since I half-expected him to say I was nuts, even though his aura looked too kindly (no harsh streaks, only gentle-looking thought forms) for that.

A more interesting illustration of the "occupational aura" is exemplified in an experience I once had at a party in Texas. A woman brought a middle-aged man across the room to me. She said, "He doesn't believe you can read auras and challenges you to convincingly read his, and he won't let me even tell you as much as his name."

We retired to a back room and I began, after warning him that I would be quite frank about what was to be seen.

He knew I had no prior knowledge of him. Anything very evidential should convince him of psychic ability, if not of auras, I thought.

The man acknowledged I was right when I told him he had a moderate case of hemorrhoids and a peptic ulcer, but responded, "But, maybe you can just tell by my face that I'm the tight-assed type [hemorrhoids] and also a worrier [ulcer]."

Maybe he thought that would ruffle my feathers (aura) a bit, but I was used to such things. So, I continued, "The intellect-related part of your aura is yellow in color—a moderate yellow, which probably means you're usually not extremely stimulated by your work. But it is very unusual, because it extends from your head area right down *both* arms, into your hands, and out all fingertips!"

"So, what is *that* supposed to mean?—that I think with my fingers and not with my brain?" the man asked rather sarcastically.

"Well," I answered, "if you were an artist, the yellow related to how you use your intellect might spill out from your head area and down one arm and hand—the one used to paint, for example.

But since your yellow of intellect comes down to *both* hands and even out the fingertips, that can mean only one thing, so far as I can imagine: You must sit using a typewriter most all day every day. I'd say you either work at a newspaper, or else you are a free-lance writer, or both."

"I'll have to admit that this is a little impressive, because I work for the *Express,* and also do quite a bit of free-lance work," the man said. "But I still don't know why that should give me yellow hands!"

Speaking generally, children's auras are almost entirely free of what, for lack of better terminology, I have called thought forms. They have not built up as many attachments and worries as adults, who are constantly confronted with diverse responsibilities. The young child's aura is usually very direct and uninhibited looking. Occasionally, on the other hand, I have seen children with auras far worse than most adults. I believe this relates to very negative behavioral patterns carried over from former incarnations.

One day a new family moved into the duplex across the street from my home. I immediately noticed that while one of the children had a rather normal-looking aura, the younger child's aura was intensely red and black. I had never seen such a thing in a child before, so I watched the two-year-old boy very closely. The terrible aura persisted for the whole fourteen months the family lived there, and the child's behavior matched it!

My wife and I became very friendly with all the family, but every chance the little boy got, he would ride his tricycle over to our house and ram dents into the side of our car.

One day while the little boy's mother was taking some groceries from out of the car into the house, the child got into one of the grocery bags left in the auto. As I watched through the window, the little boy removed a loaf of bread from the bag and began eating both the end of the wrapper and the bread. When his mother came out the door, the child threw the loaf on the ground and began jumping up and down on it. This was only typical of the many violent acts the child committed regularly.

One day while watching the child, I saw what must have been a former life, for I saw him as a man murdering someone. I know, also, from what I saw in the future of the child, that he will do it again in this life—perhaps several times.

Over and over again I have had the chance to predict a child's future by seeing the aura. I saw a friend's child when he was only five days old. That was sixteen years ago. I told close associates (not the mother and father) that the child would be in trouble with the law by the time he became fifteen, and would be confined either to a mental hospital or jail before he became sixteen. Both have happened.

In 1958 an unusual event occurred while I was riding in a car with a friend, Ed, from San Antonio, Texas. In a baby seat in the rear of the vehicle was the man's son, Mark, who was only a few months old. The baby had an exceptionally pretty aura, but as I glanced at it, a strange image flashed through my mind's eye. I suddenly saw the child at what I somehow knew to be age twelve. His aura seemed to become very weak, as if he were seriously ill. Then, just as suddenly, it came back up to normal strength.

I told Ed of the strange perception and added, "So, although I don't know how I know it, when Mark is twelve, he will suddenly become very mysteriously ill. Some may say he could die. But, don't worry, Ed, he will just as suddenly and mysteriously get well."

Mark's parents temporarily forgot about my predictive vision, and certainly never told him about it as he grew up. Yet, twelve years later, when Mark was in school, he was suddenly struck by severe and sharp pains in the chest area. Rushed to the hospital, doctors determined that a hole had appeared in one of Mark's lungs, permitting air to enter the thoracic cavity. That had caused the severe pain.

For days the boy was in the intensive care unit of a San Antonio hospital. His condition was very serious, and some felt he might die. The parents were very worried until, suddenly, Ed remembered my prophecy twelve years before and told his wife. They ceased worrying.

Within a few days, the hole in the boy's lung mended just as mysteriously as it had appeared. The cause of the malady was never determined.

So we see that the aura, or else what the mind projects as a visual symbol of things perceived at a perhaps more abstract level, can clearly reveal the future—even where that future is strange and seemingly irrational.

Philosophically, what is puzzling about events like the one I had with the baby Mark is the fact that the pattern of future events are "there" and discernible so long in advance. Anything I would say about the hows of such precognitions would be pure speculation, but it seems safe to say that the common, rather pat view of time may be in need of some revision.

The generally held concept of causation may also be in need of revision. Since becoming aware of the human aura on a continuous basis, I have seen evidence that even persons who die by "accident," and those who are murdered, have unconscious foreknowledge of their own deaths. In some cases, a part of the unconscious even seems to participate in setting up the proper circumstances for the fatal event. I know this may seem contradictory to what has been assumed to be the basic, ingrained, "will to survive." Yet, at times and in certain persons, at least, a seemingly stronger unconscious desire for death seems to take hold over the helm of the ship of an individual's life.

One evening in 1958 six young men in their late teens came to my parents' house in Corpus Christi, Texas, to talk with me about some research into the "paranormal," regarding which I had received some publicity in the week prior. I had never before met any one of them, although I'd spoken to one briefly on the phone, arranging the meeting.

Gazing across the room, something that I saw surrounding one of the youths—a healthy-looking high school senior—puzzled me, and somehow deep within it filled me with a sense of foreboding.

It was very rare in those days that I ever saw the aura—the 1957 case of the woman's envious aura (described earlier) being one of a very few instances which I clearly remember from before 1960. But what I saw could not escape my notice.

Great masses of dark or black amorphous

clouds seemed to float around the body of the youth, whom I shall call Tom. I saw very little light of any color. Somehow what I saw gave me the subjective impression of a person of terribly negative, selfish temperament, and left me feeling that the light of Tom's spiritual and mental faculties had withdrawn through an *unconscious* nonsurvival tendency. There was the added impression that Tom had a strong revulsion for someone or something in his normal, daily environment and experience, and that such a negative emotion transferred over into other aspects of his life.

As I continued to gaze at Tom's aura, being cautious not to appear to be staring at him (he looked like a very self-conscious type), I developed a distinct feeling that, although he had no conscious desire to die, the spirit that was the real, animating force behind that body was *already* withdrawing, and would leave the body *permanently* within a few days!

As such impressions flashed through my mind much faster than the time it takes to tell it, still another awareness bolted forward which seemed to show me that Tom's light of being (as I call it) was so rapidly withdrawing that in, specifically, *eight days* there would be no light left.

In other words, I seemed to know with total assurance that in exactly eight days the high school senior would be *dead* from *external* physical causes magnetized to him by his dark and negative psychological and spiritual state. Understandably I was shaken, even though Tom was a stranger to me.

So strong were my impressions of Tom's future that within fifteen minutes after my introduction to the group of youths, I asked to privately talk to the two of the six who seemed to be closest friends of Tom.

Initiating my private remarks to the two youths, whom I shall call Pete and Terry, with a stern warning not to dare tell Tom what I was about to say, I spoke bluntly and frankly:

"There is something I must prepare you to experience regarding your friend Tom. He is in a very negative psychological state which, *only eight days from today,* if not before, will attract *physical death* to him—from a source outside himself. In other words, Tom will die in eight days from something that has nothing to do with any physical sickness."

Poor Terry and Pete. They looked at me half frightened, not knowing if I were a madman or prophet. They had only known me for fifteen minutes, so their astonishment at my statement can easily be understood.

Because of the boys' reaction, I continued, "I only tell you this so that: (1) you can avoid the shock when it happens; (2) you will come to know by experience that human consciousness is capable of knowing beyond the present and even beyond the logical sequences of events, and (3) so that as a result of the total event, including Tom's impending death, you will seek more consciously to know more of your own true, spiritual nature, which I believe is capable of awareness beyond the body or even beyond spacial and temporal limitations."

The two youths then guaranteed me that they would tell no one of my prediction, but Pete added, "I still can't believe anything bad will happen to Tom. He's just an ordinary guy. There's nothing different about his personality, and he's perfectly healthy."

I once more assured them that Tom's death would not be related to internal, bodily causes, adding, "Something else will just suddenly kill him within eight days. That's all I know."

During the next two hours of the six youths' visit, Pete and Terry cast nervous glances at me and their friend Tom. I sensed that they were trying to forget what I had told them.

Before the boys left, Tom asked to borrow a certain book. I loaned it to him, but six days later drove over and picked up the book out of concern that after Tom's death within a couple of days, it might be hard to reclaim it. When I got back home with the book, there was a nasty note by Tom! "Only a goddam fool would believe this ESP crap in this book. *You're a goddam fool.* [signed] Tom." At least I had been right about the boy's negativity.

Two days later, I was beginning to feel I had been wrong, since I had not heard any news of Tom's death. Then, just after noon, the phone rang. It was my father.

"Ray," he asked, "weren't those six boys who came over to the house the other night from the Oak Park area of town?"

"Yes," I answered. "Two of them actually live on Oak Park Avenue."

"Well," my father said, "the local news report from the radio just said that a high school student who lived on Oak Park Avenue was shot and killed by his father. Then the father killed himself. I don't recall the kid's name."

Shocked, I put down the phone. I hoped sincerely that it was not Tom—that I was wrong.

With shaking hands, I dialed the police homicide division to find out who the dead boy was.

It was Tom.

I just sat there feeling ill. Not fifteen minutes passed before the phone rang again. I answered and heard the frantic, tear-choked voice of Pete.

"Ray, did you hear Tom's *dead*?" Pete sobbed. "His dad just went crazy this morning and shot Tom to death, and then blew his own brains out. I was outside in my yard. I heard Tommy scream something. Then I heard the shots. Then one more . . ." Pete broke into such sobbing that he couldn't talk.

"Look," I said, "you and Terry knew in advance about it. It might have been harder on you guys if you hadn't known . . ."

"But we didn't *believe* you," Pete said, sniffling back the tears.

Later that afternoon, Pete and Terry showed up at my place. They obviously needed comforting. Their eyes were swollen from crying.

I tried to explain to them that Tom's father had only pulled the trigger—that Tom's *own* state of mind and unconscious tendencies had clearly brought the event upon himself, as indicated in his aura eight days earlier.

"My God!" Terry exclaimed. "Now I know why you suddenly showed up at Tom's house two days ago to get the book you loaned him. *You were absolutely sure of your prediction* and wanted to get the book before it happened!"

"Yes, you're right," I said. "But I didn't want to tell you and Pete just why. I felt badly enough having to tell you what I did eight days ago."

Then I went on to assure the two boys that

death is not the end of life for anyone. "It is just one more beginning," I added.

Each time I think back upon that sad day in 1958, I recall how unbelievable my talk of seeing a human aura (Tom's) was to Pete and Terry on that first night I met them. Yet to me, auras remain sometimes frighteningly and sometimes even awesomely real, as in those instances when I see people's bodily diseases revealed clearer than by any X-ray picture. I shall next describe the appearance of specific diseases in the aura.

10

To See the Body as It Is

"So, Mrs. Stanford, the X ray clearly indicates that there is no fracture or foreign matter creating those sharp foot pains," the bone specialist told my wife. "You must have arch trouble. I have written a prescription for a special arch support which you can get."

I paid the $34 doctor bill and left the doctor's office fuming. "I'll be damned, Kitty-bo, if there's anything wrong with your arch. I'm not going to waste any more money for some prescription arch support. The auras of weak arches do not even resemble those red streaks that come from your foot's sore spot."

"Would you take a closer psychic look at my foot when we get home? You know it's been hurting me there for two years now, and I want to find out what's wrong," Kitty-bo said.

When we got home, I did take a closer look.

"Kitty-bo," I declared, "that orthopedic physician is just incompetent. The aura around your foot's sore spot looks like it would if there were some foreign matter there—like a sliver of glass, maybe from way back when you were a kid or something."

"You're probably right, Ray," Kitty-bo said. "But what doctor's going to do surgery because some guy has psychically seen a piece of glass in the foot that he can't see on an X ray?"

"I know what doctor will!" I declared. "Dr. Clark!"

"You mean *you'll* do the surgery, Ray?"

"Well, I *was* Dr. Clark, wasn't I?" (See Chapter 4.)

"If you trust yourself, I trust you too, Ray," Kitty-bo said. "But where will you get the equipment?"

I sent her brother, Sam Johnson, who was visiting us, down to the drugstore to pick up some razor blades, cotton, and alcohol.

Although I did not tell Kitty-bo, I knew that with my using crude tools and with no anesthesia, my first razor blade incision would have to be *exactly* beside and parallel with the length of what my "X-ray vision" told me was at least a quarter-inch glass sliver.

Kitty-bo assured me she had total trust in my surgical ability, so while Sam held her legs and she closed her eyes, I carefully and very quickly thrust the razor's edge into her flesh.

Then, probing the incision with the edge of the blade, I saw, about a quarter inch beneath the surface, an awful-looking glass sliver. It was pointed straight inward, perhaps into the bone.

Everytime I touched the sliver, poor Kitty-bo

jerked and complained. It soon became obvious that the larger end was the innermost one! But after forty-five minutes of work with Sam holding the legs down and a magnifying glass over the incision, I victoriously (but ever so carefully) lifted out the glass sliver, which was nearly three-eighths of an inch long. The surgery would have taken much less time had a local anesthetic been available. With Kitty-bo jerking in pain, I had to go very slowly in order not to shatter the piece of glass.

The incision healed rapidly with no complications, and Kitty-bo was overjoyed. Two years of stabbing pain had ended. "I'm sure the 'operation' wasn't as bad as having a baby," she said.

Kitty-bo seemed to remember getting glass in her foot from a broken milk bottle many years before. "The sliver must have migrated to where you found it," she said.

I thought about seeing the bone specialist again just to wave the sliver (which Kitty-bo preserved and cherishes) in his face, but figured he would never believe us—much less refund the $34.

It was not until after the surgery that I told my wife how many extra of those traumatic razor blade gashes I might have had to put into her foot if my auric vision had not revealed the exact spot in which to cut. Furthermore, I had secretly prayed that my hand would be guided to cut exactly where I must.

The glass-sliver irritation aura was an easy basis on which to diagnose, as are the auras of most physical conditions, except certain ones, the effects of which are broadly dispersed throughout the body, like diabetes. However, there was a learning period for me in which I occasionally met embarrassment.

For example, following an aura lecture in San Antonio, Texas, some years ago, I decided to actually demonstrate aura reading.

After warning the audience of "the many juicy things I can tell about anyone from the aura," I asked, "Now, is there anyone who *dares* let me read his aura?"

I always have said that before choosing volunteers to read. The reason is that only the heartiest of nonconforming individualists dare raise their hands. That type never has a dull aura, so I do not have to say, "Sorry, Miss, your aura is just too plain-Jane to be of interest."

The woman I chose was easy to read. Even the type and exact color of her automobile appeared to me in her aura! But she had something that, at the time, puzzled me a little: there were splotches of *pink* auric light all over her body.

I had already told the audience that pink means pregnancy, but that it radiates beautifully from the expectant (and sometimes *un*expectant) mother's lower abdomen—*even a few hours after conception!* I even bragged about how I had accurately told several friends they were pregnant when I saw them at work the morning after.

However, this woman's pink-splotched aura left me a little uncertain, but I described it and told her, "So, I guess I'll have to say you're pregnant. Are you?"

"I can positively assure you that I am not pregnant," was the disappointing reply.

Suddenly, and perhaps out of ego self-defense, the answer came to me.

"I've got it!" I bounced back. "The pink

splotches are the effect of taking birth-control pills. They provide *a hormonal simulation of pregnancy,* but the hormones are distributed throughout your circulatory system. That would explain why the splotches are all over."

"You're right on that one," the woman said. "I do take the pill."

Since then, observation and questioning have verified what I intuitively grasped that night for the first time. Now, I wonder if the fact that the mere presence of certain hormones associated with pregnancy can cause pink in the aura is a clue to the *physical* origin of certain aura types. Yet, we must recall that Dr. Van de Castle's "pregnant aura" (see Chapter 1) seems to have been purely mind-caused.

This subject calls to mind an experience I had in 1974 in Toronto, Canada, while I was there to lecture on auras.

A woman reporter said, "Sincerely, Mr. Stanford, I find it terribly hard to believe that you can really tell things about persons by seeing colors around them. If you can tell me anything convincing about myself, then I could change my mind."

This was a challenge I could not turn down, so I looked for a moment at her aura and knew I had it made. "O.K.," I said. "Can I be *very frank* and tell you absolutely anything I see?"

"No one can embarrass me," the self-sure reporter replied.

"All right, then," I said—probably a bit smugly. "You have a bad case of vaginitis. The aura around your vagina and even in toward the cervix shows light red-gray, glowing spots of irritation. This appearance indicates a fairly severe irritation usually associated with a yeast infection. And, since I see pink splotches all over your body, I'd say you're definitely taking birth-control pills. Your persistent use of them has caused too much moisture of the mucosa in the cervix, and hence your difficulty in ridding yourself of this bother. Then, too, your droopy, listless-looking aura looks like that of persons who don't get to bed before 1 to 3 A.M., and it must be true of you."

"Everything you have said is true," she responded. "You've just about got me believing in auras."

In an earlier chapter, I mentioned seeing a case of venereal disease. In recent years, I see it all too frequently. Most persons would be shocked at the percentage of both males and females affected with gonorrhea since the advent of the "new morality" and of "the pill." Seeing auras convinces me that people were better off before the advent of either, but maybe I am old-fashioned.

Gonorrhea makes distinctly red auric spots in the cervix, usually with a diffusion of a light red color throughout the cervical lining (mucosa) in females, and usually a more intense and generally distributed red in the urethra in males. In extreme and long-standing cases of gonorrhea, I have noticed a possibly associated reddish inflammation of skeletal joints, resembling arthritis.

A few years ago a friend of mine had been almost given up for dead after a car wreck in which his chest and abdomen had been crushed and his lower jaw literally forced into his chest.

Due to the miracles of modern plastic surgery, you would hardly have known of the fellow's misfortune by just looking at him—unless, that is, you could see auras.

One day my friend said to me, "Ray, tomorrow I go in for surgery. My doctor says there are several spots of abscess in my thorax which must be surgically removed. I don't know where they are located or how many there are, but I'd like to have you try an experiment to blow the doctor's mind. If you will, I'd like to have you take this special pen and mark an X everywhere you see an auric sign of abscess. Then when the doc cuts into me tomorrow, I will already have told him what the X's represent."

"It's no problem," I assured him, as I began to mark four X's on his chest. I placed one over each area where I saw a small but intense red light streaming out.

When my friend was back out of the hospital a couple of weeks later, he told me how things turned out.

"The doc was really skeptical when I told him how the X's got there," he said. "But when I talked to him after the surgery he admitted great astonishment. He had removed only three abscessed areas, *and you had placed a mark precisely over every one of them.* Then I asked the doc, 'What about the fourth X? Did you find anything there?'

"The doc said yes, he found some irritation there, but didn't consider it bad enough to cut out. I'd say you were a hundred per cent accurate, Ray, and the doc agrees."

"I may have been a hundred per cent accurate, but your doctor wasn't," I replied. "He should have removed that fourth area. It's got a redder glow than ever."

Just a few weeks later the doctor told my friend that he would have to go back into surgery.

"I should have gotten that fourth area the first time I went in, but hated to do it without being certain of the need," the doctor told him. "Now the X ray shows it to be worse off than the former three areas. I have no choice now."

The surgery was successful. My friend and I both wished the doctor had been able to see auras so that he could have completed the job the *first* time. In fact, if I ever try to teach any people to see auras, it probably will be medical doctors, especially surgeons. They could make constructive use of it.

I usually try not to usurp the province of physicians, unless they ask me to help, as has sometimes happened. Yet, one night in Corpus Christi, Texas, I was talking to a medical doctor and his wife, whom I had only met that evening, when I noticed something I felt it necessary to mention.

In the lungs of the doctor's wife I noticed three spots of whitish-gray light that I well knew to be associated with the calcium and scar tissue the body builds up in the lungs around tubercular lesions.

"Please don't let me frighten you," I dared to say to the woman, "but I see colors around people. The colors and shapes reveal physical conditions of persons' bodies to me."

The doctor looked at me like he thought I should be hanging from a walnut tree, but I continued. "I see two light, whitish-gray glowing spots in your left lung, *here* [I pointed] and *here*. There is another one in the upper part of your right lung, *here*."

The doctor's jaw dropped noticeably. The woman responded, "You can see my husband is shocked. But it's because you're right. Some years ago I had double pulmonary tuberculosis. I've still got three spots of scar tissue that show up clearly in X rays. They are exactly in the three places where you pointed."

"If I didn't know better," the doctor said, smiling for the first time, "I'd say you've seen her X ray."

One time I was asked by a psychology professor at a university to come and read auras for the entire psychology faculty and their assistants! Admittedly, I was slightly nervous—not due to any worry about failure, but because some psychologists can be very nasty regarding such things as aura seeing. Some years earlier, one psychologist, upon hearing that I claim to read auras, said to me, "Oh, come on! Only a damn fool would claim to be schizophrenic." I would have had the last laugh if I told him that I knew about his bleeding, herniated hemorrhoids! Such persons do not bother to *test* those of us who actually see auras.

Anyhow, I accepted the offer to demonstrate to the psychology faculty, under the condition that the professor who arranged it bring several bottles of wine to pass around. That would get everyone "loosened up" while I was still explaining about colors and thought forms. Then by the time I got around to actually reading auras, the imbibers should have lost some of their inhibitions, and their auric secrets should really hang out!

The plan worked reasonably well, and by the time I got down to the aura reading, most of the professors had become less negative and were viewing the whole thing more as a game.

Sometimes I see things it would not be polite to mention—not in a group, anyway. That was the case with a girl's aura I read that night. She was a student assistant to one of the professors.

Vibrations in the red rays from the girl's genital system did not look like VD, so I could not decide exactly what to say about it. I simply described what was seen, adding, "So this means there is some at least temporary disturbance there, but I'm unsure of its exact nature."

At first the girl said, "I don't know what the trouble could be." That bothered me because I felt she was not being truthful.

"Are you *quite* sure of that?" I insisted.

"Well, I *am* in the first day of my period, if that's what you mean," the girl admitted.

The professors seemed to agree that might well be a "hit."

There was something else I did not dare say about the girl, considering her reluctance to even talk about being in the first day of her menstrual period: The auric emanation from vagina to cervix looked highly irritated, as if almost abraded. As I later told the professor who invited me, "Her vagina looked *worn out*—like she normally wears it out having sex several times a day."

"I'm sure you're right!" the psychologist said knowingly. "She was introduced to you as a teaching assistant. Well, she *assists* her professor all right. It's common knowledge—probably even to the professor's wife—that he puts the screw to his assistant at *least* once a day. The whole psych department knows that. There's no telling who else she services, either. There's not a professor there who wouldn't have believed you if you'd said she had a worn-out 'vag'!"

That same night I deliberately chose the most skeptical person present to read his aura. The premed student and teaching assistant acknowledged with true astonishment that I was right when I told him that his aura revealed to me that he daily stood before a computer as if working on it, was born in Hawaii, was brought up near a large fresh-water lake in the Midwest, and composed music regularly.

He was convinced and happy with what I saw and said, but I would like to have seen some *physical,* bodily condition to diagnose. Fortunately for him, he was in perfect vitality, so there was nothing to do but give him a clean auric bill of health. He had not even shown any auric signs of using drugs, hallucinogenic or otherwise.

Auric signs of drug use have become something of increasing concern to me over the last sixteen years or so. The ways in which such substances as LSD, heroin, etc., alter and distort the human aura are shocking and even frightening to see. Even marijuana use has its unmistakable telltale auric signs. It might be instructive for me to verbally illustrate those effects. So, at the risk of offending some users, I shall now describe the symptoms precisely as I see them so clearly every day of my life that I leave the house. I speak of frightening auric syndromes that are now displayed with unprecedented frequency among the population at large.

Quite some years ago I began to see highly strange conditions in some persons' auras that I had never seen before. As in the case of the pink blotches of birth-control pill takers, it took me a while and some questioning to realize the meaning of the observed changes.

The aura of the regular pot smoker is not nearly so abnormal and distorted as those of users of strong hallucinogens and narcotics. That is not any justification for continued marijuana use, however, since the attendant changes are normally not positive ones.

As a person begins to smoke pot frequently, the *movements* of thought forms within the aura *slow down*. This suggests to me that, while the pot smoker may be getting less uptight about some of the stressful life circumstances encountered, the capacity to effectively and quickly handle some challenges may also be slowed or lessened.

The pot smoker's aura seems to be, for lack of better terminology, *lulled,* if he or she has had at least a few hits on a joint recently.

Then, too, the normally bright auric colors (except the "angry" reds and blacks), including the yellow of intellect, seem to become slightly less brilliant. The colors do not seem so outreaching or radiating, as before usage was begun. In fact—and some persons laugh when I describe this—the auric colors literally seem to become *hazed as if by smoke!*

Under the influences of marijuana, the aura that formerly showed a capacity for rapid mutation of color and form becomes like a person trying to run in water—a slowed-down churning effect.

The confident pot user will interpret this auric observation in his own way, but to me it signals a lessened capacity to act in a maximally purposeful and effective way within the environs of modern, Western society.

LSD use affects the aura in a much more distinctive and even frightening way.

At first, after say one or two nonextreme acid

trips, obvious changes occur in the "timing" and intensity of thought forms. The effect is almost the opposite of that seen in pot smokers: A person who was not formerly inclined to show drastic color and thought-form appearance and disappearance begins to have quick and intense changes in auric colors and thought-form patterns—changes that "burst" into existence in the aura.

Such a person may decide that those first acid trips have caused the mind to become more spontaneous, more creative, more aware of reality's vast diversity and potential. I should not be bothered if the changes were to stop with those effects, but if usage of LSD is continued the changes become more extreme.

In describing the chronic aura mutations that occur with continuing use of acid, let me ask that the reader imagine that all the aura colors and thought forms I have hitherto described anywhere in this book are somehow transmitted out of the surface of the body through (and displayed *in*) a solid glass atmosphere or environment. The colors and forms become visible and move rather smoothly in the high-quality glass. Now, take a sledge hammer and produce abundant fractures of that glass within several feet surrounding someone. You can imagine how refractively *distorted* and *complex* the resultant auric images would become.

That is exactly what happens to the appearance of an aura in the second stage of acid use. When I described this to one audience, an acid fan jumped up and shouted, "Why don't you just come out and *say* that we acid heads are all *cracked!*"

"*You* said it, brother, I didn't," was my reply, but it did bring to mind the fact that some researchers use LSD to create a chemically induced schizophrenia in research subjects.

It is not difficult to imagine how strange and puzzling this "cracked" aura appeared to me when it first made its appearance in public over a decade ago. Is it any wonder that real acid heads have trouble being objective, collecting their thoughts and "getting it all together"? Their auras are perfect pictures of a disintegrative and distractive mental state.

What I call "acid aura disintegration, stage three," is even more disconcerting. The person who has been using acid rather frequently for months or even several years shows not only the "cracked" aura, but actual *holes* in the aura.

The holes are usually a quarter-inch to (in severe cases) several inches across. They are surrounded by red and muddy, murky mixtures of violet, brown, green, yellow, etc. When one acid head asked me to describe his aura to him "as it is," I said, "I don't enjoy telling you this, but your aura looks like some guy ate too much split-pea soup and barfed it up, along with his stomach ulcers, all around your head!" (The poor guy stopped acid tripping—for all of two weeks, that is.)

Actually, the chronic acid user's auric holes have a frighteningly ugly "something" about them that is even more *sensed* than seen. I refer to the actual *black* areas themselves, and not to the awful colors bordering them.

My subjective impression of the black holes is that they seem to open into some terrible, cataclysmic, extra-dimensional "space," the entry of consciousness into which might cause total dissolution of even the soul itself—a metaphoric "outer darkness" where the only real contact is with absolute, permanent, and total emptiness.

In the early 1960s, before LSD was generally outlawed, a then-famous psychiatrist from California visited me in Phoenix. The doctor operated a special school and home for so-called exceptional (brain-damaged, etc.) children. The doctor's physiognomy was that of the hyperthyroid, nervous, neurotic type. But the moment the doctor walked in I knew from his aura that he was an acid head. He informed me that he was *regularly* administering LSD to many of his young charges. "It helps them freak-out and experience something different than their ordinarily boring, traumatic lives," he said in justifying the procedure.

Then the psychiatrist really laid it on me. "Ray, you say you haven't taken LSD yet. You should. *Soon*. It's too important an opportunity for someone like you to pass up. You know, within only a few months of LSD use, I have become like *Jesus!* I *am* the Christ, in fact. I have also attained oneness with the Buddha, Krishna, Sri Ramakrishna, Saint Francis, and others."

I looked once more at the doctor's aura. If that is what the apostle meant when he wrote that Jesus' "countenance increased and became radiant as the sun," then the twelve disciples must have been jiving around Palestine wearing rose-colored glasses! Instead of divine or saintly, the famous doctor's aura looked more like that of a highly neurotic cat on a hot tin roof.

Another thing that shows up in the hard drug user's personality and aura is paranoia. The aura and thought forms begin to radiate and move in suspiciously convoluted patterns that sometimes temporarily conceal a highly explosive red anger-aura within. The auric yellows are often tinted with *browns* in paranoids. In persistent cases of such toast-colored auras, the person gravitates almost exclusively to brown and/or gold clothing. I believe the wearing of more colorful clothes could even assist some paranoids to become more positively outgoing and open in personality.

In late 1962 still another well-known psychiatrist from California visited Arizona, where I lived at the time. This doctor had become famous for his involvement in court cases where the accused person was claiming insanity.

The psychiatrist became well known in Arizona for something entirely different. For $75 he would take you on a personally guided acid trip. He never offered me such an "inward venture," but many of my acquaintances had "journeyed" with him.

I had noticed not only the typical and ugly signs of chronic LSD use in the doctor's aura, but an abundance of convoluted forms, along with the toasty brown tinges of paranoia. As a result I was not surprised when the doctor (a somewhat likeable sort, otherwise) asked to have a "secret talk" with me in which he promised to reveal "the world's most immediate menace."

The psychiatrist had learned that within a few days I would leave on a trip to Egypt, Lebanon, and five other Mediterranean countries. So, he felt it important to tell me about the "secret menace" and solicit my aid.

"Ray, you are psychic enough to know that what I am about to reveal is absolutely true, so I will not try to prove my point," the doctor said confidently. "During an acid trip recently, I was walking on the beach near my home in California. Suddenly, a voice spoke powerfully within me. It said, 'Humanity's most potent enemy is *right beside you!* It is right there in the ocean. Look!' "

The doctor explained that as he gazed at the surf, he noticed a subtle glow within the waves. "*There they were,* Ray. Teeming billions of billions of photoplankton and plankton—dividing, multiplying, filling the ocean and *ready to invade man!*"

I could not imagine what the doctor was getting at, so he explained. "Look, I'm sure you know that the salinity of the blood is almost exactly that of sea water. *The plankton menace is migrating from the seas into our bodies!* It has been revealed to me that they are the major cause of aging, impotency, mental-emotional disorders, many types of cancer, and a vast number of other human problems."

"Aside from the question of whether or not blood-born plankton could cause the things you have named or not," I said, "I seriously doubt that, even if plankton could enter the bloodstream, they could live very long in the human body."

"Oh, but, unfortunately, they can, Ray," the doctor declared. "And I'll show you the *proof!*"

At that, the doctor went to a mirror, located a blackhead on his nose, and squeezed the core out onto his finger.

"See!" the psychiatrist announced triumphantly. "Here is a plankton that migrated from a capillary to near the surface of my nose. *It's a frightening thing to think about!"*

Then he said, "I want you to carefully record the water coloration at various places in the Nile you visit, and also in the Mediterranean Sea, and report back to me. I can thereby calculate the population density of the plankton menace in that part of the world."

This was just one more example of the pitiful state to which the minds of normally brilliant persons can be reduced by dangerous use of LSD and other consciousness-altering drugs—quite aside from the corresponding nastiness of the personal aura that results. Auras, remember, are only the *effects* of consciousness and bodily conditions. They are not the cause of awareness, but its visible "reflection."

It seems appropriate to mention here that in my seventeen years (since 1960) of seeing auras in everyone I have encountered, I have not seen even one single aura which gave evidence that positive, permanent, objective alteration of consciousness and positive growth in personality and spirituality had occurred through drug use. In fact, just the opposite has been the case. The only personal aura improvements observed have been in persons who have genuinely sought to manifest love to their fellow beings and to some Principle higher than themselves, call it God or whatever—it is not what it is called, but the outlook that seems to matter.

Interestingly, the auric changes for the better (brighter, more outflowing, fewer thought forms hovering around) have never been seen in persons who pay fancy fees for "self-improvement," "spiritual development," "control-the-mind," "ESP development," "aura reading," or even "White Brotherhood" courses. Perhaps the lesson here is that the road to hell can be paved with good intentions of teachers and/or students. It seems that one cannot *buy* spirituality, which my experience suggests is synonymous with love.

How, then, does one improve one's own aura? First, not by wanting to merely clean up *appearances,* which the aura is, but by positive transformation of *consciousness* in body, mind, and spirit, of which the aura (whether objective, or only projective and symbolic of things sensed intuitively) is the effect. Persons who pray and meditate without getting onto any ego high horses, and who do so *without* making psychic powers (but rather God) the goal of those prayers and meditations, are the ones who become more real in the process.

As for those persons who have gotten consciousness into an oppressive state with drugs like LSD, heroin, alcohol, etc., they must begin just where they are. There are no shortcuts. If the mind is so subjective that one cannot still it in meditation, then prayer, good diet, exercise, and persistence of good purpose seem to provide the most direct route out of the drug-induced morass.

I mentioned *alcohol* as a consciousness-altering drug. While its effects in limited use are not so dangerous as substances like LSD, chronic usage is both physically and literally depleting.

Late one night I peered into a cocktail lounge. While several pitiful humans drooped over their chemical somas like wilted flowers praying before some altar to the god of thirst, awesome and ugly psychically visible forms hovered menacingly nearby. Like the lower spirit that followed the aspiring medium with an injured back, just to suck the red energy being emitted, so did those even more unwholesome and subhuman "things" seem to draw on the uglier colors surrounding the bodies of the alcoholics.

The energies of escapist fears and resentments actually expand as muddy-colored light from intoxicated persons, oozing food for psychic things which are so ugly that if most persons could see them, they would never want to see auras again—much less drink alcohol to any extreme.

In some cases, I have known the psychical "feeding" of lower entities and their thought-form bodies to become so severe that the "thing" got hold of the mind of the drunkard. Maybe I am old-fashioned, but it looked like *possession* to me. It is more than alcoholically released hostilities (normally repressed) that, in some cases, cause intoxicated persons to commit heinous crimes, like killing a beloved friend or even a total stranger. From psychic observations I know it is sometimes actual possession by an outside psychic agency that provokes those deeds, although I believe this is relatively rare.

But what would be the *motivation* of the "possessing" entity? some would ask. My answer: Psychic "food"! A person being threatened with a knife or gun, roped, or having a knife plunged into the chest or throat, gives out vast quantities of psychic energy that can feed not only the possessing "thing," but a whole host of its psychic playmates!

I can see a whole host of psychologist and psychiatrist readers laughing their heads off at such a dark-ages statement. But I challenge such persons to a contest of picking ten chronic alcoholics out of a room of one hundred persons, by looking at the *backs* of their heads. The typical psychologist or psychiatrist would be lucky to locate one of the alcoholics. I can locate most of them by seeing the auras and the attracted "things."

The prospects are not too good, but some skeptics might even learn to see auras someday. That is one of the topics of my final chapter. But first I shall answer some unanswered questions.

11

Some Answered Questions

From time to time, questions have been asked concerning my experiences in seeing the aura. The best ones have been presented to me in written form by my friend John Palin, a mathematician who is interested in understanding psychic phenomena. Some readers have likely wondered about many of the same things, so I now shall share some of John's interesting questions and my answers.

"Can you see auras on TV?"

I watch TV only a few times per year, but have never seen an aura on the tube. Yet, if I attune what I might call my "inner knowing self" to the person being seen on either live or taped TV, in my mind's eye I can clairvoyantly see (or else imagine?) an inward awareness of that person's aura at the time. There has been very little opportunity for me to test such indirect aura "seeing" objectively.

"Can you see auras in the mirror?"

Yes, my own included, but the aura image is backward, just like all other things are in a mirror.

"Can you see auras at night?"

Of course I can, but something in my conditioning that says, "One does not see as clearly in darkness," seems to dim the auric vision just slightly.

"Can you therefore locate a person hiding from you at night—hiding behind a tree, say—by auric vision?"

It is seldom I have the chance to try that. On the few occasions it has been attempted, I have been successful.

"Is there a fundamental, prevalent difference between the auras of human females and males?"

Yes, there are some subtle differences, unless the female is exceptionally masculine, or the male exceptionally effeminate in personality. For example, a very effeminate person displays more auric gracefulness with curving, flowing lines of thought form. Masculinity in the aura seems to be characterized by more straight, assertive forms and colors. Also, whether one's auric thought forms reach out to embrace an attractive female or male is often an indication of one's sexual orientation, if not of one's sex. I have never seen a male, regardless of how effeminate, emit the "champagne" (auric bubbles flowing upward from the eye or eyes) described in an earlier chapter.

"Does the aura penetrate barriers like walls, etc?"

Yes, it can do so. Often, the ability to penetrate

such barriers seem related to the personality of the person displaying the aura. It may even reflect that person's conscious or unconscious world view.

"Do animals have auras? If so, do they differ fundamentally from human auras?"

Animals very definitely have auras. Basically they seem less complex depending on the species or the character of an individual within a species. Fish, for example, have very simple auras—basically physical looking, with occasional emotional reds. There seems to be very little sign of intellect.

On the other hand, dogs sometimes display highly varied auras. A few canines show remarkably humanlike emanations. I have a friend who has a standard poodle bitch with an aura that remarkably resembles that of an old-maid school teacher I once knew!

"Can the aura be photographed or measured in some way?"

I know of no successful photographs of an ordinary human aura. However, from early 1968 through early 1971 a total of more than two million persons witnessed (and many *photographed*) the apparition of a "lady of light" moving around the roof of a Coptic church in Zeitoun, Egypt. Some of the well-authenticated photographs of the apparition show something indistinguishable from a rather exceptional and nice human aura around the glowing woman. Many observers felt "the lady" was Jesus' mother, for it was the church of St. Mary at Zeitoun where that phenomenon was repeatedly seen, photographed, and authenticated by an official investigative committee appointed by the Egyptian government.

If camera film can be described as measuring the human aura, and if the "lady of Zeitoun" was human, then perhaps the aura can be measured.

"Do the people you know who see auras have anything in common other than auric vision?"

So far as I know, only in that we all display what psychologists might call "highly visual" personalities. That means that we tend to notice and respond more readily to colors and forms in our environment than other persons.

"Does a person's aura remain fairly stable or individually distinguishable over an extended period of time?"

Although most persons' auras change constantly, the basic, predominant colors and thought-form characteristics of individuals seem to remain fairly persistent—even over many years in some persons. In other words, even though persons change moods temporarily, the basic, underlying personality structure is not readily mutable.

"Does drunkenness inhibit or help your aura seeing? How about the affect of other physical conditions?"

Never having been drunk, I cannot answer the first part of the question. But I suspect that some aura seers, if slightly "high" from alcoholic beverage, might become less inhibited, and hence more accurate, in *interpreting* what they see. I would not consider that a good excuse for excessive drinking, however.

I know of no physical condition that helps aura seeing, per se; but there may be some unknown to me.

"Do a person's color or clothes-color preferences influence that individual's aura?"

That is difficult to evaluate or know, since a person's basic personality influences both his or her color preferences and auric emanations. In my experience, the color of clothes a person is wearing is *not* a reliable index of aura color.

"Will the color in a room affect the aura of a person who enters that room?"

In most cases, not immediately. Yet, if a person comes into a room of very soothing, relaxing colors—such as certain shades of green or blue—after a while the aura will "relax." The hovering thought forms will lessen, the auric change or thought-form motion will slow down, and the aura will become nicer in appearance— although not necessarily blue or green.

Still other colors, especially color combinations in a room, can actually stimulate the intellect and, hence, increase the intensity of yellow in the aura. Research on the effects of color environment upon growing children suggests that an environment of nice, bright color combinations can actually stimulate the child's intelligence quotient (IQ) in a positive way. So, in the long run, yellow in the child's aura would become more intense.

"There has, in recent years, been propounded a theory of 'personal space.' That theory suggests that, depending on personality variables, individuals have 'personal space' barriers. If another person comes within the radius of that personal space, its owner becomes uncomfortable or agitated. Does this correlate with the bounds of an individual's personal aura?"

Actually, in some cases, there may be an *inverse* relationship between the aura and "personal space." For example, many criminally inclined persons and assorted paranoids and "red neck" types usually have very *large* personal spaces upon which one dare not "trod." Yet, such individuals often display very "tight" auras. That is, their auras are highly *intense,* but drawn in close to the body as if explosive energy were being confined in a container that could explode with only minimal stimulus.

On the other hand, friendly, outgoing persons often have large, nicely radiating auras, while their personal space is quite small. You can come very near, physically, to such persons without disturbing or angering them.

It may be that in criminals, paranoids, etc., the aura is actually drawing in for fear of "touching" persons. In the nice, friendly person it may be actually flowing out, almost as if "to touch" others.

"Is the aura of a sleeping person any different than when the same person is awake?"

The aura "relaxes" somewhat during some periods of sleep. Thought forms diminish. It becomes more peaceful. But when dreaming occurs, the aura becomes more active and varies with the dream content in a way resembling the active aura of the wakeful state.

"Do you see the aura all the time, or do you have to look for it—like looking for a speck on the wall you know is there?"

I certainly do not have to look for the aura. It sometimes even jumps into my awareness with an almost hyperdimensional reality. But, I sometimes have to search inwardly for the *meanings* of what I too easily see.

"Do you see the aura all the time, or do you have to look?"

Yes, I see it all the time. But I have built the

habit of trying to avoid becoming auricly aware of the problems of others.

"If a person imagines his aura to be expanded, does it actually expand?"

Sometimes as a temporary thought form, yes. But it is difficult to fake a big, generous aura.

"Can one consciously or unconsciously shrink his aura by being guarded about his thoughts and emotions?"

To some extent, yes. But it is difficult to keep up one's guard all the time.

"Can one cause one's aura to completely cease to be visible to an aura seer?"

Yes, that can be done, but only by the few who know how. I did that once as a test when a well-known and very honest aura seer was trying to read my aura. He responded, "This is very strange, but you are the only person in whose aura I can see absolutely nothing. It is almost as if I were somehow blind to your aura—and yours alone."

It is difficult to explain by what process of consciousness I can "blind" others to my aura, and I am not sure I would tell how if the words could be found. But there surely must be others who can do the same.

"Can one see the aura by taking drugs?"

Not so far as I know. One might fool oneself by taking a drug that expands the pupils, preventing perfect focus at certain distances. Then, one might mistake unfocused objects or persons as having an auric "fuzz." But that is hardly the aura.

"Is the aura as viewed from the side different from the front or back view?"

Yes, indeed. Auras seem to be suspended

151

within three-dimensional space. Hence, you can view them from all sides, but not simultaneously unless you have a rather remarkable clairvoyant ability.

"Can you tell much more about some persons by way of the aura than about others?"

Yes, that happens. Some persons have very plain auras that tell me little. They are usually the ordinary "plain-Jane" type. Outstanding persons usually have highly telltale and remarkable auras.

"Have you ever seen an aura that was not associated with a physical body, such as around an astral body or ghost?"

Yes, I have. The "ghost boy" who visited me in Phoenix, for example, had an aura, but I do not recall paying much attention to it.

"Does a highly creative person have a different aura from a more ordinary person?"

Of course. The auras of creative persons are much more animate than those of uncreative individuals, even though the latter may be highly intelligent or intellectual.

"In the years you have seen auras, have you noticed any changes in the auras of large groups of people? Have auras at large improved, deteriorated, or remained the same, generally?"

It is difficult to make a generalized evaluation of aura changes collectively over the past fifteen years or so. The superficial aspects of auras generally seem to have worsened—probably through use of drugs, excessive TV watching, and other escapist pastimes. At the surface, auras are, by-and-large, more confused, fragmented, muddy-colored, and disturbing to see. However, I've also noticed that a deeper strength seems to be arising subtly in many persons. I prefer to refrain from making any cut-and-dried value judgment of what I see collectively. Oddly, some of the more pleasant auras I see are *not* those of the "truth seekers." But maybe that is because those who are reasonably peaceful and in harmony within their lives are not compelled to seek spiritual needles in haystacks.

"Are there any circumstances when you cannot view the aura as well as usual—in a room lit by ultra-violet lamps, or by red or blue lights exclusively, or by very harsh white lights? Does moonlight or polarized light affect your aura seeing?"

Certainly my aura seeing, as well as my normal seeing, seems slightly impaired when I am very tired or sleepy. Otherwise, I cannot think of other impairing conditions. Even the rooms illuminated exclusively by such frequencies or intensities of light as those mentioned do not seem to affect it very much, unless my eyes get naturally tired. Generally I try to avoid prolonged exposure to weird lighting. It surely is not soothing to the eyes. Moonlight or highly polarized light have never seemed to alter my auric vision.

"Do eyeglasses—which I note you often wear—help your seeing auras or the details of thought forms?"

Yes, they seem to make the *details* clearer and to keep the aura colors from blurring together. If aura seeing is a projective (subjective) phenomenon instead of an objective one, then the glasses may help only psychologically because I know I can see normal things better with them. On the other hand, maybe they do focus auric light, but I find that a little difficult to believe.

"What percentage of persons would you say see auras?"

If the question refers to *unconscious* aura seeing, the answer may be that *all* see auras. If only "highly visual" persons see auras (which I doubt) even unconsciously, the researchers in that area of study would have to supply a percentage figure of how much of the population is highly visual.

As to *conscious* aura seeing, the figure would be extremely low, especially when we eliminate all the *imagined* aura seers who have taken phony courses that have only taught persons to mistake disfocus and retinal retention phenomena for auric vision.

I would guess that far less than one hundredth of one per cent (less than one out of ten thousand) of the population are really consciously seeing auras. Tests with children, to date, seem to have been too "leading" to get a true percentage figure on aura seeing by children. Youngsters can really let their imaginations run wild when they think a teacher or researcher wants them to report that they see colors around persons. It may well be true that more children than adults consciously see auras, but great caution should be exercised in approaching the question with children.

Finally, my friend John Palin asked me, "Has this aura seeing made you different from other persons? In dealing with people, has this made you like a gambler who may feel he knows beforehand what the outcome of a situation (but in this case an interpersonal one) will be?"

I cannot say that it has made me feel very different from other persons in most ways. At times, however, it may cause me to feel and experience certain things more intensely or consciously than most persons.

Seeing the auras of others does make me more conscious, I believe, of the need to recognize how my thoughts, attitudes, and actions may influence the consciousness of others. On the other hand, I cannot say that it has done anything to make me more able to actually *do something about* that sense of responsibility!

The gambler comparison is not entirely inappropriate. I can often tell well in advance how persons will react or interact. A highly personal example comes to mind. It occurred shortly before my wife, Kitty-bo, and I were married in December 1972. We had seen each other only three times prior and had never dated.

Kitty-bo just looked at me and suddenly said, as if out-of-the-blue, "Ray, are we going to get married?"

Although I hardly knew Kitty-bo, I had inwardly attuned with her and had also observed her aura. I knew her to be a very good person who felt deeply about me. So, I casually said, "I guess so, Kitty-bo." A few days later we were married and have never regretted it.

All psychics aside, I did not need ESP or auric vision to answer that question in the affirmative. I had told a mutual friend a few days earlier, just after I had first met Kitty-bo, that she was the most beautiful girl I had ever seen. He said he could say the same thing. I would have been a real fool to say "No," or even "I don't know," to Kitty-bo's question. I did not need any confidence to answer her in the affirmative. But had I needed it, my inner feelings and auric vision provided all the evidence I needed. Thus, auras sometimes even help me answer important *personal* questions when they are asked.

12
And So

I had just completed a talk on apparitions when a well-dressed, middle-aged woman walked up and declared, "Mr. Stanford, I just loved your talk, but your aura was even more fascinating than what you said!"

The psychic personality is said by some researchers to be an outspoken type. Since that definitely is true of myself, I almost had to bite my tongue to keep from responding, "Well, in that case, next time I'll save my voice and just silently stand there for people to scope out my aura," but discretion took over and I asked instead, "What is so fascinating about *my* aura?"

"The whole time, Mr. Stanford, it just glowed a gorgeous, simply *gorgeous,* glowing *green,*" the lady said in her sweet southern drawl. "It was so simply *resplendent* that you must have been divinely, just *divinely* inspired! I'd even say you're a *healer!*"

I could not believe it. I had always thought that only true, natural healers of real ability would show such an aura as the obviously sincere lady was describing.

"Oh, I can assure you my aura isn't that nice," was my response. But, realizing she might think I was just trying to appear humble, I added, "Only someone like a powerful healer has that kind of aura, and my wife will tell that when she has a headache I'm *not* that."

At that point another woman broke into the conversation, saying, "She's *right*. I saw your aura, too. It was just the color of my bells of Ireland flowers—but, *oh,* so alive and glowing!"

"Now, I assure you," I said jokingly, "that my aura is probably just too much for color TV. But like a bell of Ireland, it isn't. I see it in the mirror every day. I've never seen any nice greens in it."

Then a third woman's voice from behind me broke in.

"Then how come *I* saw it too—just the same as they did?"

The three friendly women were just about to launch me on an ego trip, when I happened to notice the brightly lighted curtain in front of which I had been standing during the lecture. It was a radiant orange-red color. I knew, with some degree of relief, what had caused them to think I had a deep, bright green aura. (An aura like that would be just too much responsibility for me to be wearing around.)

I explained to the three women that as they stared at me in front of that brilliantly illuminated orange curtain, the eyes had tired and shifted slightly from one side to the other, continuously. This common fatigue effect, together with retinal retention, creates an optical illusion that resembles a glowing region one to four inches wide around an object at the distances they had been from me. In this case, because the brightly lighted background was orange-red the eyes saw that area as the spectral complement, a radiant green.

"Stare at the microphone and podium for a minute," I challenged them. "You'll see they have that beautiful healer's aura, too!"

"Oh, my gosh!" the lady who started it all exclaimed. "You're right."

"But my aura-reading teacher told us to stare at anyone that way with a nice lighted background," one of the women complained. "She said that's the way you see the aura!"

"How much did you pay for the course?" I asked.

"Two hundred and forty dollars," the embarrassed woman replied with growing remorse.

"Well, you just got ripped off two hundred and forty dollars to learn to misinterpret optical phenomena," I said. "Had the curtain been red, you'd have sworn that I had a radiant blue aura."

"I'm afraid I took a course by the same woman," another of the three confessed.

I sympathized, telling the women that during my travels around the country, I have encountered thousands of well-meaning persons who have been taken for a financial loss by phony aura seers, who are either genuinely self-deceived or should be sued for deliberate false advertising.

"Before I signed up for the course and paid my money, this teacher told me that there was no chance of failure," one of the women said. "I would be able to see colored auras around people by the end of the first session, she promised."

Of course the phony teacher could promise that! She knew all human eyes behave in pretty much the same way, and that most people are unaware of the illusions that can be so easily produced.

In *New Horizons*, the journal of New Horizons Research Foundation, Toronto, Canada (Vol. I, No. 3, January 1974), Doctors A. R. G. Owen and G. A. V. Morgan describe and explain experiments by Owen that conclusively demonstrate the nature of the effect I have been discussing— which they call the *rim effect.* The article does not mention the rim effect one gets with brilliant, highly colored backgrounds, but does thoroughly expose the rim effect seen even on backgrounds that are not brightly lighted or very colorful. It would be nice if some agency could require aura teachers to have their prospective students read the *New Horizons* article and related literature dealing with color-compensatory and perception mechanisms of the human eye. There would be a lot less money and time wasted.

The fact is that anyone who really sees the auras well enough to easily perceive verifiable and unobvious facts about total strangers, also surely knows that *aura seeing cannot be easily taught.* I would go as far as to say that, if it can be taught at all, it can only be easily learned by *visually oriented persons.* All of the persons I know who can really see the aura are *artists* (myself included), except Fred Kimball. And while not an artist, Fred is so visually oriented that when I visited him, I found his mobile home walls were covered with beautiful, iridescent tropical butterflies which he had collected in his travels.

When you go to a person's home and the walls are colorless and bare, you can know the person who lives there is definitely not visually oriented. Such persons are very unlikely candidates for seeing auras. If the reader finds his or her home that way, just save your money if someone offers you an aura-seeing course.

While I do believe that some persons might be taught to see auras, I am dubious of all the courses I have ever heard about. None of the aura teachers I have ever met could see anything other than optical effects and the products of their own imaginations.

Those persons who *really* see auras know that the emotional challenges of actually seeing other persons' illnesses and feelings could not be easily handled by most people. For that very reason, I have never known of a true aura seer to offer courses, despite all the claims and noise made by the self-deceived Johnny-come-lately (a $50 to $2,000 course later) "psychics," and fast-buck artists who can be found lurking behind the door of half of our nation's metaphysical bookstores.

Beware of believing any person claiming to see auras who has the subject sit in front of a white or specially colored screen. Some "readers" go as far as to have you change into white, black, or specially colored clothing. If they need that kind of help, it is not auras but optical effects and illusions they are seeing and teaching you to see.

Also, beware of appliances sold with the claim that they will enable or aid you to see the aura. "Aura goggles" are one ridiculous example. It is true that they allow you to see certain optical effects, but these effects have about as much resemblance to the aura as Kirlian photography.

It is amazing to me how many writers have, without question, taken Kirlian photographs to be actual pictures of the human aura. It should have been obvious from the start, since a Kirlian "aura" cannot be photographed unless a high-energy field is applied to the object or person's body part being photographed, that what is recorded is coronal effect and not the human aura.

Some Kirlian fans will object to my statement, countering that the photographed effect varies with the mood, health, etc., of the person being photographed. Some Kirlian photos have been interpreted that way, but one should be aware that electrogalvanic skin response and the chemical content of the blood also vary with mood and health, causing the corona being photographed to vary.

Is there no hope, then, that auras shall ever be seen by large numbers of persons? some will ask.

Not so many years ago, it was generally believed (even by some parapsychologists) that so-called ESP or, more generally, *psi phenomena,* were special "gifts" available only to the "chosen" few. Extensive experiments of very thoughtful design have dispelled that fallacy. It is now known that all persons are engaged in psi function in almost every facet of daily life. Some persons use it, unconsciously, against themselves (maybe they enjoy self-pity), while others use it consciously and unconsciously to aid themselves.

It probably is the same with auric awareness. Most or all persons probably "see" them unconsciously. It is just that persons with a high degree of visual orientation most easily become aware of the phenomenon. (And please be aware here that my statement has nothing to do with whether aura seeing is an objective or projective form of psi function.)

By using techniques like, say, training "visual personalities" to consciously *notice* colors that normally are only subliminally seen, I might teach persons who have a high degree of need for auric vision (surgeons, for example) to develop an awareness of that which I believe to already be seen unconsciously. (The latter statement is based on the widespread use of figures of speech such as "green with envy," etc.) I suspect that those persons who have a need of or constructive personal application for auric awareness in their daily lives are about the only ones who could psychologically cope (effectively) with such experiences.

Of course, this book would sell better if it offered auric-vision techniques that everyone could easily apply. But think of the psychological traumas and immense responsibility it would place upon the aura viewer. What married man, for example, could handle the temptation of knowing exactly to what degree women other than his wife are desiring him. I would ask the same of wives. This is only a highly simplified example. The real effect and responsibility would be devastatingly greater in most cases. I would not want to be responsible for putting such a psychologically heavy load upon the unprepared. I'm not looking down my nose at the inabilities of others to cope with auric awareness. This is a realistic appraisal based on years of observing auras and asking myself whether it would be constructive or destructive for most persons to see into the lives and personal secrets of others.

Despite all the potentially negative ramifications of aura seeing, it can have its values in family life, interpersonal relationships, etc. Grudge holding, for example, is obvious when the aura is seen, and might be subjected to the light of constructive open discussion.

Auric vision provides an experienced observer with a highly accurate assessment of the psychological development of an individual, which could be especially valuable in the early phases of child rearing. A negative pattern seen in the formative stage could be a lot easier to modify than one of long-standing manifestation.

Aura seeing could be immensely helpful to law-enforcement officers. One ready application would enable the officer to know what to expect of an arrested person: If the red of the aura tends to flow to and out of a hand, the person is likely to slug or pull a gun on the policeperson. If it tends to flow out to or from the mouth, then the officer may only be told off, or at worst, spat upon. The way in which a person tends to vent anger is clearly evident in the human aura.

Juries could always hand in just verdicts if they could see auras. Judges could hand down more just sentences, I believe.

Almost any day I walk down a certain street in Austin, Texas (or any major city, for that matter), I can spot one or more murderers. Occasionally they carry a guilty thought form of the victim(s). But, what am I to do in a time when even the hands of law officers and judges are tied by criminal-favoring technicalities?

The reality of reliable psi function poses some

interesting challenges and questions for the whole field of criminality and law enforcement. I am convinced that many successful criminals use unconscious (and sometimes conscious) ESP in committing their crimes, and I suggest that law officers learn to do likewise in fighting crime.

Aura reading on my part has proven very helpful to my close friends. I can detect their physical problems even before the doctors have noticed the ailments. The ability has proven one hundred per cent reliable in disease detection—even in seeing the condition weeks or months before it was detectable by conventional diagnosis. Almost all disease conditions are more susceptible to treatment when nipped in the bud.

In an earlier chapter I mentioned warning business friends about persons of bad auric presence and of the unfortunate situations that have occurred when my warnings were ignored. If auric vision were widespread, honest business persons could deal only with persons with honest-looking auras, while criminal types would shy away from dealing with anyone who showed an honest aura! Nice, pure colors would let the criminal know that such a person would not knowingly join in on a dishonest deal. Auric vision could become a two-edged sword.

In business I recommend that employers employ only persons of similar or *complementary* auras. The latter enables a boss to hire persons who display traits lacking in the business firm. I always apply this principle in hiring at the offices of the Association for the Understanding of Man. Someday maybe I will be accused of *aura-color* discrimination! But I do not worry too much.

That would require a *legal recognition of auric existence,* which would please me very much.

Aura seeing might prove very helpful in the classroom. For example, a teacher could tell just by looking at the aura whether or not a child's problem was a matter of lack of intelligence or of some emotional nature. (By evaluating the quality, intensity, and shape of the yellow—intellect—in a person's aura I can usually evaluate that individual's intelligence quotient accurately to within five points.)

By way of thought forms, an aura-seeing teacher can tell if a child (or adult, for that matter) is just throwing up temporary and arbitrary mental blocks to listening and learning, or whether the problem is more deep-seated.

Likewise, it would be easy for the aura seer to know quickly whether problems between two children are seated deeply within their unconscious mechanisms, or whether they are only temporary.

In these times of change, many young and older persons alike are exploring diverse "new" religions and seeking gurus of every sort—fat and skinny, verbose and silent, discreet and indiscreet, holy looking and unholy looking. If they could see the auras of certain gurus, there would be a lot less bowing, scraping, and foot kissing. Yet, some of them have a lot nicer auras than others.

I have met numbers of gurus and sat-gurus over the past sixteen years, but in early 1971 I met one who displayed an auric phenomenon I had not anticipated.* When the distinguished,

---

* Some followers choose to imply that their guru is better than some other types, hence "sat-guru" or "true guru."

white-turbaned gentleman walked into a private room in the San Antonio airport, accompanied by a host of his devout followers, the room became filled with the most beautiful white auric light I had ever seen. It seemed even to penetrate every otherwise dark corner of the crowded room. I was immensely impressed. Surely one such as he, in whose presence the room became filled with pure white love and light, was a living saint, a man in whom God truly lives.

My second observation of the aura of the sat-guru bothered me, however. On that occasion I saw him heading into a rest room when no followers were in sight. I was shocked. There was none of that beautiful love and light. In fact, the man's aura looked disappointingly ordinary, except that it was nicer than about ninety-five per cent of the auras I see.

By careful observation a bit later in that same hour at the airport, I was able to solve the mystery: When the sat-guru was with his followers he was as, by analogy, a sphere with tiny mirrors glued all over it. The intense and sincere love and auric light from each of the many disciples was being reflected by the sat-guru. With seventy-eight devotees around him—loving him, cherishing him, and intensely beaming their individual devotion to him—it was no wonder that the room was filled with far more auric light than I had ever seen! It only *seemed* to come from the turbaned man. Out of the devotees' sight, his aura was only a bit better than that of anyone of his most devoted followers. He provided only a focus and mirror for the disciples' own love.

But then the philosophical question arises as to whether or not the sat-guru was *responsible* for the love those followers were able to radiate so beautifully. I asked a follower about that, thinking he might be taken aback. He was not; and he replied, "Oh, *Master* is the source of all Love! Of course he conceals *his* love, but only to make us *yearn* for it. He reveals it secretly in our own hearts so that we may truly learn to love through loving him."

Even if I could have, I was not about to argue with an answer put so sincerely and beautifully. Yet, it seemed to me, knowing some of the disciples, that their problem was in loving *only* their "master" and having disdain for all the rest of the world and for all persons who had not been wise enough to accept initiation by their sat-guru. Somehow I feel that the Master of masters would obviously be capable of giving direct love, instead of just reflecting it. Otherwise, where is the *example* toward which we are to grow? The disciple's answer was just too convoluted for me to swallow. But it was beautifully and sincerely stated.

I have been in groups of other devotees in the presence of their guru, but none of the other gurus seemed able to evoke such sincere and intense love and devotion for their "master"—if auric light is any indication. Fanaticism and groupie-type following is another thing, but it does not display itself as nice, white auric light—only in silly, fanatical grins and attempts at proselytizing.

Then there is the guru whose aura has the habit of massaging the breasts of his prettiest female disciples. When I told this to some friends, one asked, "Do you have any way of knowing if it ever descends to the physical?"

"I'm not absolutely sure," I replied, "but that guru himself said in a talk just recently, 'As above, so *below'!*"

I hope no one takes what I am saying wrong. There are some good people teaching spiritual laws and exemplifying them. It is just that all of them are human in one way or another, and what their auras reveal has so far kept me from going overboard with admiration for very long. Whether a guru's auric armor has been gold, silver, pewter, or lead, to speak figuratively, I have not yet seen one that does not have a simply human chink in it somewhere. But then, everyone else's does too, including my own. I suppose emotional needs determine who or what one worships.

My own aura seeing has given me no indication that one type of worship is absolutely superior, but, rather, that it is *hypocrisy*—and not one's religion—which can destroy people. This seems to be confirmed by the fact that Jesus, for example, never preached against *any* religion. He just preached against *hypocrisy*.

Love, however, seems to be the most important ingredient, whether to a beautiful aura or to, more importantly, a beautiful *person*. One thing that can strangle love and, in turn, beauty, seems to be uptightness—taking anything and everything *too* seriously. Many a saint, and Jesus too, has laughed even in the face of death. I suspect that if God laughs, He laughs at how seriously people take their misunderstandings of Him—not that *I* understand Him, but at least I fancy that if God has human characteristics, I give Him a good belly laugh every now and then!

I know that if I am uptight, it is not as easy to

understand the meaning of auric forms seen. In the same way, uptightness blocks off our conscious attunement with the inner, spiritual nature. I have never seen a nervous-looking, uptight aura that showed great radiance and inspiration. The most magnificent auras seem to appear around persons who show a beautiful balance between "innerness" and "outerness." These persons are not the type to resent outer challenges or even troubles. They are not escapists, as are those who pretend to renounce attachments to worldly things while really only *denouncing* and resenting such things through fears of ineffectiveness.

I try, if often fail, to view the world through *Letting* (maybe that is why I so liked the Beatles' song "Let it Be"), which requires a bit of being able to laugh, even if at oneself; through *Loving* (which requires no explanation except to those who mistake lust for it); and through *Living* life to its fullest. I try to let those three L's serve as the kaleidoscopic, triangular mirrors through which I view the world and that myriad spectacle of color and form which the rich diversity of human (and even nonhuman) consciousness projects onto the spinning wheel of life.

All this calls to mind the most beautiful human aura I have ever seen. I could hardly believe my eyes because that beautiful, radiant, resplendent white aura, tinted ever so gently here and there with rose and coral hues, came from a simple little girl of fourteen who lived in Mexico. Known as a healer, she gave water to a severely epileptic baby who had come with my friends and me, and the child was completely and permanently healed

(I say this because the baby has been without epilepsy for the four years since our visit).

The little girl gave love to each of us, and through her simple gift we came home saying that for the first time we knew that God was alive, well, and working through a simple child.

The little girl left us with a message that somehow lingers long after: "Tell them that they should not come seeking me, but only the Love which God gives. Those who are healed are not healed by me. It is faith, a gift which they allow from God, that makes them whole."

It is no wonder, then, that I sometimes experience in all-too-human impatience when people come to me saying, "It would be such a divine gift, Mr. Stanford, if I could see auras just as you do."

Instead of the kaleidoscopic *eyes*, which God has given me for reasons which surely only He knows, I sincerely hope that each person instead, prays for a kaleidoscopic *heart*.

Thereby, the gift of love shown to others can match the hue of their own hearts, speaking a language that does not even dream of the existence of barriers and of impossible things.

I was humbled by the experience my wife had during one of my public lectures on the aura. It taught me that, to really speak to people, we must know the language of their own hearts.

In what Kitty-bo felt to be one of the most interesting parts of my lecture, a man, looking very unhappy, got up and left the building.

Following him outside, my wife asked in her sweet Dallas, Texas, drawl, "Pardon me, sir, but did something Ray said bother you?"

"Well," the man replied, "I don't think I'll ever

see any auras. If I *should* ever see them, it wouldn't mean much to me anyway."

"Oh! I should think it *would*," Kitty-bo responded.

"Not to *me*," the man said over his shoulder as he walked toward his car. "You see, *I'm color blind!*"